HOW TO BE A BETTER... SERIES

Whether you are in a management position or aspiring to one, you are no doubt aware of the increasing need for self-improvement across a wide range of skills.

In recognition of this and sharing their commitment to management development at all levels, Kogan Page and the Industrial Society have joined forces to publish the How to be a Better... series.

Designed specifically with your needs in mind, the series covers all the core skills you need to make your mark as a high-performing and effective manager.

Enhanced by mini case studies and step-by-step guidance, the books in the series are written by acknowledged experts who impart their advice in a practical way which encourages effective action.

Now you can bring your management skills up to scratch *and* give your career prospects a boost with the How to be a Better... series!

Titles available are:
How to be Better at Giving Presentations
How to be Better at Managing Change
How to be Better at Motivating People
How to be a Better Communicator
How to be a Better Creative Thinker
How to be a Better Decision Maker
How to be a Better Interviewer
How to be a Better Leader
How to be a Better Negotiator
How to be a Better Problem Solver
How to be a Better Project Manager
How to be a Better Teambuilder

Available from all good booksellers. For further information on the series, please contact:

Kogan Page, 120 Pentonville Road, London N1 9JN
Tel: 0171 278 0433 Fax: 0171 837 6348

how to be a
better...
leader

Rupert Eales-White

KOGAN
PAGE

YOURS TO HAVE AND TO HOLD
BUT NOT TO COPY

Kogan Page Limited
120 Pentonville Road
London N1 9JN

British Library Cataloguing in Publication Data

A CIP record for this book is available from the British Library.

ISBN 0 7494 2594 6

Typeset by JS Typesetting, Wellingborough, Northants.
Printed in England by Clays Ltd, St Ives plc

CONTENTS

■ Contents ■

PREFACE

The goal of this book is that, by the end, you know what is required to be a 'better' or more effective leader and have completed an action plan to improve your performance in this role.

Here is an outline of the contents of each of the chapters.

1. Understanding effective leadership

The starting point is to develop understanding of what is required of an effective leader. To achieve this objective, we start by putting leadership into the work context, consider roles we fulfil at work and the relevance and importance of the leadership role. We then consider the experience of those we lead – our followers – in effective and ineffective leadership. We also look at what leaders consider are the keys to success and from this establish the requirements of effective leadership, the focus of leadership in the modern business world and the connections between good and bad leadership

2. Maximizing flexibility and choice

In the second chapter, we develop the theme that we are more effective as leaders if we recognize that we have options as to which style we use, so we can choose one that is appropriate to a given situation and competence level of the follower. Completing a short questionnaire determines the extent to which we have a controlling, supporting or team orientation, from which our current leadership style can be determined. What is more, by getting a work colleague to complete a copy of this questionnaire, we can determine the extent and direction of any gaps in perception between our own view of how we lead and that of another.

3. Eliminating perception gaps

This leads to the next chapter, which considers the potential of perception gaps to limit our effectiveness as leaders. Also, how they arise and how there can be gaps between our behavioural intent, its actual manifestation and the impact on the follower, and, most importantly, what strategies we can put in place to reduce or eliminate them.

4. Motivating staff

The fourth chapter focuses on the critical need for effective leaders to motivate staff, and outlines strategies, based on research, and models of effective motivation that we can deploy.

5. Questioning effectively

We not only need to know how to be more effective, but how we can develop core skills and techniques, the application of which will enable us to get the best business performance possible from the individuals and teams we lead. In the first of three chapters on skill development, we focus on the skills of effective questioning, considering examples of ineffective questioning, determining what questions to ask and how to ensure we ask the right questions to develop both the follower and the relationship.

6. Listening actively

In this chapter, we consider why listening is important, why it is difficult, how to recognize poor listening and what we need to do to be effective or active listeners.

7. Developing creativity

Here we focus on five techniques based on question combinations that will enable us, as individuals, to be more creative and innovative, as well as developing creative thinking and an innovative approach in our followers.

8. *Improving staff performance*

With all these skills in place, we next examine the key areas we need to focus on to improve business performance. We look specifically at how to ensure our followers focus on the key areas of their jobs, prioritize their work flows and have in place performance standards, to act as a basis for monitoring, review and producing continuous improvement.

9. *Building a team*

The main focus of the earlier chapters has been on the leader's relationship with the individuals they lead. The most powerful and motivational unit, both to maximize business performance and produce accelerated development of the individual, is the effective or high-performing team. In this chapter, we look at the nature of an effective team and what a leader needs to do to build one.

10. *Reacting to change*

This is the first of two chapters dealing with change, as we all live in a world of accelerating change, with all the opportunities and uncertainties that change produces. Here, we consider how we react to change and how we can help the individuals and teams we lead to achieve maximum growth in the change process.

11. *Understanding your change preferences*

How we and others prefer to manage change has a significant impact on our effectiveness. In this chapter, you need to complete a simple questionnaire that identifies your preferences when managing change. Having explained what it all means, we consider how you can play to strengths most effectively, develop compensating strategies for weaknesses, manage relationships better and help both the individuals and the team you lead to manage change successfully.

12. Reviewing and planning

The final chapter looks back, reviewing and summarizing the key messages from the earlier chapters, and looks forward, asking you to spend a little time in reflection and planning – planning to be a better leader.

Rupert Eales-White

UNDERSTANDING EFFECTIVE LEADERSHIP

In this first chapter, we put leadership into its context, looking at the roles we adopt in the workplace. Next, we develop a model of effective leadership and consider the implications.

WHAT ARE OUR WORK ROLES?

Professor Drucker developed a model of job roles. What he suggested is that any job of work involves the carrying out of four work roles and it is helpful to any employee to put work activities and skills deployed into a role context. By explicitly recognizing what role we are carrying out at any given moment in time, we can know what particular skills we should be using and, therefore, carry out the role more effectively than if we simply dip into a generic tool-bag to carry out all our work activities.

The roles are shown in Figure 1.1, and we will examine each role briefly before making some general points.

The four work roles identified are leadership, followership, technical and administration. Let us look at each of these turn.

Leadership

This book concentrates on how we can be effective in the leadership role. Whether supervisor, junior manager, departmental manager, senior manager or executive, we have a responsibility

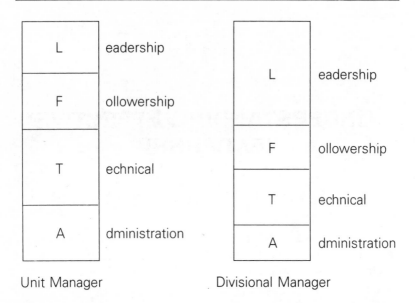

Figure 1.1 *Work roles and the variation in the mix for different jobs*

and a duty to lead those we are put in charge of as effectively as we possibly can. We explore the nature of the leadership role in depth from a practical and action-oriented perspective. However, for many in a leadership role – which starts as soon as we are put in a position of authority over another member of staff – there is no exploration, because there is no explicit recognition of the role.

For those of us who do not consciously think of ourselves as leaders and so cannot plan to act effectively whenever we carry out the role, of necessity, we tend to focus on the job or ourselves and not our followers. Nevertheless, we provide, without thought or control, a pattern of behaviour and approach that, subconsciously, sets boundaries on the motivation and performance of those we are not consciously leading. We can often be surprised at poor performance and low motivation (when uncovered by some staff attitude survey), not realizing that we are the cause of such negative effects.

Such outcomes tend to be quite common when large organizations carry out staff attitude surveys, assuming that those who fill them in believe they cannot be identified (the same holds for 360-degree feedback on the boss). The key reasons are:

❑ lack of recognition by the key decision makers of how crucial the leadership role is in the changing times we all face;
❑ if the importance of effective leadership is recognized in order to achieve cultural change, it is the absence of training or the presence of training that is ineffective;
❑ if the training is effective, there is no support afterwards – what is termed the 'glass ceiling effect' – our bosses remain as they were and sometimes do not appreciate the followers' more proactive approach.

On an optimistic note, we have enormous power as leaders to create – via the deployment of effective approaches, attitudes and skills – subcultures that transform the competence and motivation of our followers, irrelevant of the cultural norms in the company or our own boss' leadership style.

We are in a leadership role whenever we communicate with a 'subordinate', whether electronically, by telephone, in one-to-one meetings or 'team' meetings. If you were to carry out a time-and-motion study, you would find that you spend a lot of the working day in this vital role – how much time is likely to be much more than any initial estimate.

Followership

We are also followers or in a 'subordinate' role. I will use that pejorative term as well as the term 'boss' as the words are so prevalent across many countries and cultures.

If leadership training is scarce, followership training is non-existent. We learn how to be a follower by absorbing the culture and modifying our behaviour, depending on our understanding, interest and political skill, according to the unwritten rules we pick up along the way.

As Robert E Kelley said, 'Followership is not a person but a role, and what distinguishes followers from leaders is not intelligence nor character, but the role they play. Effective followers and effective leaders are often the same people playing different parts at different hours of the day'.

For those of you interested in considering the follower role in more depth (and how effective we are can determine whether or not we are promoted ahead of the pack or escape the next 'downsizing'), his *Harvard Business Review* article is excellent (see the Bibliography at the end of the book).

The key message is that effective followers:

❑ manage themselves well;
❑ are committed to the organization and to a purpose, principle or person outside themselves;
❑ build their competence and focus their impact for maximum effect;
❑ are honest and credible;
❑ think for themselves;
❑ are assertive and energetic;
❑ are risk-takers, self-starters and independent problem solvers.

Additionally, you might like to read Chapter 9 of my book *Ask the Right Question*, which looks at how to relate effectively with the boss (see the Bibliography at the end of the book).

Again, key strategies/actions suggested are:

❑ do not think of a boss as a boss;
❑ remember your boss goes to work to do a good job;
❑ recognize the existence and impact of perception gaps;
❑ develop a positive attitude to your boss;
❑ never criticize your boss;
❑ keep your boss informed;
❑ apply the PBA rule (anyone is persuaded if they perceive a balance of advantage for them in the proposition);
❑ bring your boss solutions, not problems;
❑ promote discovery with your boss;
❑ wait for the first reminder (selectively – recognizing that bosses can change their minds);
❑ always ask the right question in the right way.

We carry out the followership role whenever we interact with our boss or bosses (if we are in a matrix structure) or more senior staff, whenever we attend a meeting as a team member and so on.

Technical

The technical role is our business role, when we carry out activities that define our professional competence, whether as lawyer, architect, consultant, product manager, production supervisor, salesperson, strategic planner, business development manager, administrator, IT manager, and so on.

It is the role where we are set hard measurable targets, and is usually perceived as the most important role by the corporate culture and individual manager. The combination of a focus on the technical role and absence of training in the leadership role explains why so many managers are poor delegators and work very long hours to less than optimum effect.

Administration

This final role is self-explanatory. Our working lives are full of administration matters. We have to organize ourselves and deal with the large volumes of paper and electronic information that result from being part of an organization.

How can we use the model?

The four core roles define any job. However, the role mix varies depending on the job itself. A research scientist would have a very large technical role, a managing director a very large leadership role.

As suggested, it is very helpful to think in terms of such roles, all of which we are likely to carry out more than once in a working day. The two key reasons for this are as follows:

❑ We can identify the skills requirement of each role, the degree of overlap and degree of separation. We can devise and implement a plan to maximize our competence in each role. The lack of separation into roles has reduced the perception of importance of the 'soft' roles of leadership and followership and overemphasized the importance of the 'hard' technical and administration roles, with a severe reduction in personal and corporate effectiveness as a result.

When did you last produce, never mind, update your action plan to be an effective follower and leader? I have little doubt that you have and review regularly your action plan to meet your business targets.

❑ We can identify which work activity slots into which role, and therefore apply the skills or competences appropriate to that activity. It is a good idea to develop a role mind-set, to recognize when we are switching roles and what is the appropriate mind-set for that role. Often, we can leave a meeting as a follower, feeling frustrated or angry and, without pausing for thought, vent our anger on a subordinate, only to regret it and apologize. If we consciously recognized the switch in roles, we would have tempered our approach to our own follower and been a more effective leader as a result.

WHAT CONSTITUTES EFFECTIVE LEADERSHIP?

Having put leadership into its context, let us consider what constitutes effective leadership. We are going to look at this from three perspectives:

❑ a follower's view of good leadership;
❑ a follower's view of bad leadership;
❑ a leader's view of good leadership.

A follower's view of good leadership

We want you to get a pencil and paper, pause for a few minutes and consider your own personal experience of leadership. Think of specific individuals in your life and times when you have been in the 'followership' role. You do not need to make it work-specific, but think of *all* kinds of individuals – parents, teachers, 'gang' leaders, lecturers and your bosses since starting work. Think back and think of any action each individual took that you felt helped you in whatever way. List all the different actions, focusing only on what was positive for you.

We do not know what you have written, but we have asked this question of many groups of managers from many companies and different cultures. It is surprising just how much commonality of thought emerges from very personal experiences. We will take the answers from a group of managers working in the insurance sector as an example. We have restructured the list into four key action areas and then set out the specific actions suggested in Figure 1.2.

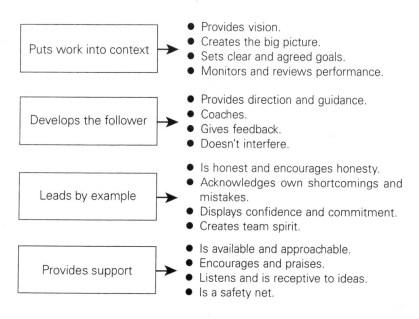

Puts work into context	→	● Provides vision. ● Creates the big picture. ● Sets clear and agreed goals. ● Monitors and reviews performance.
Develops the follower	→	● Provides direction and guidance. ● Coaches. ● Gives feedback. ● Doesn't interfere.
Leads by example	→	● Is honest and encourages honesty. ● Acknowledges own shortcomings and mistakes. ● Displays confidence and commitment. ● Creates team spirit.
Provides support	→	● Is available and approachable. ● Encourages and praises. ● Listens and is receptive to ideas. ● Is a safety net.

Figure 1.2 *What an effective leader does*

This list is action-oriented and, at first glance, appears insufficient. For instance, good leaders motivate their staff. However, when we look at motivation, we will discover that it is necessary and sufficient to carry out actions within this set to motivate staff. The other factor is 'analysis paralysis'. Many organizations spend months trying to develop a complete set of what are termed 'leadership competencies' and then define each competence by a complete set of behaviours, skills and attitudes. When they come to train and develop according to this list, they find enormous overlap, because the competencies are not mutually exclusive. They are often incompatible (decisive leader and effective teambuilder, for example) and, in any case, it is impossible to achieve all these desired behavioural outcomes.

We should always be mindful of a quotation by Brian Pitman, Chief Executive Officer of the UK financial institution Lloyds TSB: 'Strategy is focus and hard choices'. To become more effective leaders, we need to select key actions and then focus on making them happen.

Turning now to your list, how does it compare?

Another question. Which of the list of 16 actions do you feel you are incapable of carrying out? When I ask this question, invariably all the managers say 'At a pinch, we could do them all.' The list and the answer lead to two basic conclusions.

❏   You manage tasks, and lead people. Often managers can make poor leaders, as they try to manage people as if they were tasks – impersonal entities to be organized, directed, controlled and monitored.
❏   We can all be good leaders. Actions speak louder than words. If we do the right things at the right time in the right way, we will all be brilliant leaders. We can become leaders – we do not have to be born leaders. The model of heroic leadership – the charge of the light brigade – is, or should be, long dead.

A follower's view of bad leadership

Now, repeat the previous exercise, but this time focus on everything that demotivated you, upset or annoyed you – accentuate the negative from past experience.

Again, I do not know what you have put on your list, so will share a list generated by a group of managers, this time working for a Malaysian multinational.

They said that bad leaders were dictatorial, inconsistent, failed to involve the team or set clear objectives, criticized and rarely praised, had favourites and showed prejudice, failed to delegate or simply dumped, failed to listen or provide feedback, showed no respect, were intransigent and closed-minded, failed to communicate results, did not give support, and did not appreciate their followers or their followers' workload.

Again, there is a core of commonality, and a very large core, when different groups of managers from different companies, industries and countries respond to the question.

Interestingly, when asked the question 'Which of the actions of a bad leader (in a worst case scenario and having crossed your heart to tell the whole truth and nothing but the truth), would you not be capable of committing?', what do think was the reply? You have got it, 'none'.

Every individual is capable of the actions of a good *and* a bad leader. As Thomas Carlisle said, 'The ideal is in thyself, the impediment is in thyself also.'

So, it is not a question of becoming a good leader by trying to follow some externally developed prescription, but discovering the effective leader in yourself. What you can achieve is continuous improvement, more and more occasions when you behave effectively as a good leader, and fewer and fewer occasions when you behave ineffectively as a bad leader.

The remaining chapters of this book focus on the critical areas and provide tools, techniques and stratagems to accentuate the positive aspects and minimize the negative aspects of your natural leadership abilities.

A leader's view of good leadership

I have not looked at the view of good leadership from the perspective of the leader for two reasons:

❑ your opinions will now be coloured by your reflections;
❑ when asking groups of managers to go into syndicate rooms, each with their own brief, so that their thinking is not affected, the conclusions of the group looking at effective leadership as leaders mirrors very closely the conclusions of the follower group sharing their experience of good leadership.

We all know what it takes to be effective. The real question is what do we need to do to be effective – how do we go about being a better leader? The answer to this question is the focus of the next ten chapters.

2

MAXIMIZING FLEXIBILITY AND CHOICE

You may have noticed that in Figure 1.2, What an effective leader does, in the last chapter that by 'Leads by example' was 'Displays confidence and commitment', and by 'Develops the follower' were 'Provides direction and guidance' and 'Doesn't interfere'.

If we are to display confidence and commitment as an effective leader, then we need to develop the right attitudes. The first part of this chapter examines how we can do this.

Now we cannot provide 'direction and guidance' and 'not interfere' at the same time. Effective leaders know when to do what with whom. In essence, we have to adopt different aspects of our leadership repertoire depending on the situation we face and the competence and maturity of the team or individuals we lead. There is not a single leadership style nor approach that is applicable in all cases, so, in the next part of the chapter, we look at what your current leadership orientation is. From this we can develop a model of leadership styles, and then examine where you fit in and what choices are available to you to maximize effectiveness.

DEVELOPING THE RIGHT ATTITUDES

There are some key aspects to this – attitude to the leadership role, to yourself and to the individuals you lead. We shall look at each of these in turn.

Attitude to the leadership role

We looked at this briefly in Chapter 1, but let us now look at it in more detail. Too often we focus on the many tasks we have to complete and targets we have to achieve – on the technical and administrative roles. We tend, as a result, to be 'managers of staff', not 'leaders'. Effective management is all about planning, organizing, coordinating, directing and controlling. However, people just don't like, generally, to be planned, organized, coordinated, directed and controlled! As the American billionaire Ross Perot put it, 'People cannot be managed. Inventories can be managed; people must be led.'

The fundamental objective of effective leaders is to get the best business performance they possibly can out of the people they lead. This requires a focus on, as we have seen, putting the follower's work into context, developing the follower, leading by example and providing support. So, we need to develop a very positive attitude to the leadership role, recognize how crucial it is and that we need to consciously think and plan to be effective on a regular basis – focusing on those activities that will produce the best performance from the people we lead.

We may need to consciously do some 'unlearning' to develop the right attitude to our leadership role. Many people from many different cultures have a mind-set concerning what the core of leadership is all about – a view often developed from childhood experience as a follower. The view is that a leader should be in charge, should be seen to be in charge and should make all the decisions, as the 'buck stops here'.

This view is deeply held by most, I would suggest, and I have seen the reality expressed on many occasions. I still recall a group of executives developing their leadership, teambuilding, team-working and change management skills by completing a series of structured activities in an outdoor environment. With the first task, for which the team had 20 minutes to succeed or fail, we nominated a leader and, within seconds, the now followers were saying 'Over to you boss. Tell us what to do', and the leader was manfully (in this case) trying to work out what should be done. They completely failed, and during the review, the executives began to develop an understanding of what effective team leadership was all about. By the end, whoever was appointed 'leader' was coordinating a ten-step process to achieve success. The power of process and the leader as process coordinator is looked at in Chapter 7.

Attitude to ourselves

As noted earlier, we are all capable of being poor leaders or good leaders. One of the reasons for our being able to display many of the behaviours of poor leaders is that we have a poor attitude to ourselves. When we lack confidence, feel insecure (deep down), do not have a high sense of self-worth, we will spend our time focusing on ourselves and trying to remove these feelings to meet our own needs. We then have no time for our followers and will try to manage them using 'command and control' as a permanent leadership style as that takes the least time.

Effective leaders focus on their followers, not themselves. So, we have to consciously develop a positive attitude to ourselves, recognize and dwell on the many strengths we all have, build our self-esteem, calm ourselves down and consciously and deliberately start to switch focus.

When we have managed our own psychology, developing the right attitude, then a practical manifestation of our new approach (where it is a new approach) will be to start regular team meetings and one-to-one meetings. This provides time in our busy diaries for those we lead. Once we do this, we will end up saving time as the more effective our followers are, the less busy we need to be.

Attitude to our followers

Many years ago, a colleague told me a true story. A large group of schoolchildren were selected for an experiment. There were ordinary, 'average' kids. They were split into three smaller groups, say, A, B and C groups. Each group was given a teacher to educate them. Each teacher was told a different story about the children. Teacher A was told that he or she had been given a group of highly gifted, well-behaved children, teacher B a group of run-of-the-mill kids and teacher C a bunch of poorly behaved no-hopers.

Six months later, each group was behaving exactly as the teacher had been told to expect. The results and behaviour of group A were brilliant, group B average and group C dire. Thus, just as we need to develop a very positive attitude about ourselves and our abilities and potential, we need to have the same thoughts about each and every individual for whom we have been given a leadership responsibility. This can be extremely difficult indeed, but unless we think the best, we cannot hope to get the best.

WHAT IS YOUR LEADERSHIP ORIENTATION?

Figures 2.1 and 2.2 are two simple inventories, each consisting of 36 statements.

Figure 2.1 is for you to complete. You decide whether you agree or disagree with a given statement and put a cross in either the 'Agree' or 'Disagree' box. A decision must be made for each statement.

The second inventory, given in Figure 2.2, has the identical statements, but this time the answers are to be given by a work colleague whose views you trust – and not a follower as, for cultural reasons, they may not be totally honest. The same simple procedure as you used for Figure 2.1 should be followed by him or her. Remember he or she is putting their view of how you operate in a leadership role at work.

Once both inventories have been completed, you can proceed to scoring. The way this is done is shown in Table 2.1. Taking your inventory, look at the three 'Self' columns in Table 2.1 and circle those numbers where you have put an 'Agree' and only an 'Agree' in your inventory. Put the totals of the numbers circled at the bottoms of each of the three 'Self' columns, for 'Controlling', 'Supporting' and 'Team'. You then end up with a set of three numbers, which in the example given in Figure 2.3 is (4, 10, 8). You can make a graph for your numbers in the same way as is shown in Figure 2.3 by filling in the blank version shown in Figure 2.4.

If we call the individual in our example shown in Figure 2.3 Charles, the maximum is 12, and so Charles sees himself as low on 'controlling', very high on 'supporting', and high on 'team'.

If you repeat the scoring for your colleague's answers, filling in the 'Other' columns in Figure 2.4, you will get a complete picture, including the extent and location of any differences of perception.

In the case of Charles, his 'Other' profile is (8, 6, 4). So, he is seen as strong in 'controlling', moderate in 'supporting' and low in 'team'. The differences are −4, 4, and −4. In Charles' case there are significant gaps between how he sees himself as a leader and how he is seen. We devote the next chapter to how such gaps can arise and, more importantly, how they can be eliminated.

Before using the data provided to consider leadership style, I shall set out the broad interpretation of different profiles, looking briefly at profiles where there is agreement (no or a one-point difference) and then where there are perception gaps.

Where there is correlation

Dealing with 'team' orientation first, the higher the score the greater the ability to build an effective team. If the score is very low (say 3 or less), and especially if you are high in 'controlling' and low in 'supporting', I would recommend you find some way (perhaps a short external programme, open to other managers from other organizations, and so with none of your colleagues in attendance), where you experience effective teamwork. This will provide you with both belief in teams and the ability to build an effective team yourself.

If you have moderate to low 'controlling', moderate to high 'supporting', and moderate to high 'team' scores, then you have all that is required to build an effective team.

If you have very low 'controlling' and very high 'supporting' and 'team' scores, you may have problems with decision making. During teambuilding, you need to control the process. Afterwards, you need to make decisive interventions, when some change has disrupted the team dynamics. (See Chapter 10 for more detail on this.)

Excluding the 'team' dimension, if the scores for 'supporting' are very low (3 or less) or those for 'controlling' very high (9 or more), the implication is that you are too oriented towards

Leadership orientation: your own perception

		Agree	Disagree
1.	I regularly check that my staff do what they say they will do.	☐	☐
2.	I care about colleagues' feelings.	☐	☐
3.	I believe teamworking is the best way to benefit from different individual approaches.	☐	☐
4.	I find time to listen to colleagues' concerns and problems.	☐	☐
5.	I ensure that targets, objectives and performance standards are agreed by the team as a whole.	☐	☐
6.	I discipline a member of staff who makes mistakes.	☐	☐
7.	I ensure that most decisions are made by the team as a whole and not myself.	☐	☐
8.	I keep my staff under control.	☐	☐
9.	I am quick to praise another for their good performance.	☐	☐
10.	I am quick to criticize others when they make mistakes.	☐	☐
11.	I am trusting and trusted.	☐	☐
12.	I prefer to be part of group creativity sessions rather than thinking creatively alone.	☐	☐
13.	I provide emotional support to colleagues.	☐	☐
14.	I am a coordinator rather than controller of my team.	☐	☐
15.	I find that if my staff are told exactly what is required and why, they will agree to do it.	☐	☐
16.	I prefer to work in a team rather than on my own.	☐	☐
17.	I use my authority to ensure that staff meet their targets.	☐	☐
18.	I have well-developed listening skills and am a good listener.	☐	☐
19.	I encourage individuals in the group to share their feelings and expectations.	☐	☐
20.	I develop a caring and supportive environment.	☐	☐

21. I believe that, when necessary, the judicious use of threats will get agreement. ☐ ☐

22. I promote colleagues' ideas and suggestions as well as my own. ☐ ☐

23. I persuade individuals in the group to share information and support each other. ☐ ☐

24. I persuade others with the use of my authority and appropriate rewards and punishments. ☐ ☐

25. I provide regular feedback to my staff on their performance. ☐ ☐

26. I like to be in charge. ☐ ☐

27. I help others create a shared vision and understanding. ☐ ☐

28. I prefer working with a team to working with an individual. ☐ ☐

29. I recognize the need to be sensitive to colleagues' feelings. ☐ ☐

30. I discipline poor performers. ☐ ☐

31. I believe that the best agreement is when both sides win. ☐ ☐

32. I push my views strongly. ☐ ☐

33. I usually carry out communication and feedback in a team context. ☐ ☐

34. I make my staff aware that I mean what I say, so they do what I request. ☐ ☐

35. I openly express my thoughts and feelings, and encourage my staff to express theirs. ☐ ☐

36. I am a catalyst and facilitator rather than a commander of my group. ☐ ☐

Figure 2.1 *Inventory to record your own perception of your leadership orientation*

Leadership orientation: another's perception

He or she...

		Agree	Disagree
1.	regularly checks that members of their staff do what they say they will do.	☐	☐
2.	cares about colleagues' feelings.	☐	☐
3.	believes teamworking is the best way to benefit from different individual approaches.	☐	☐
4.	finds time to listen to colleagues' concerns and problems.	☐	☐
5.	ensures that targets, objectives and performance standards are agreed by the team as a whole.	☐	☐
6.	disciplines a member of staff who makes mistakes.	☐	☐
7.	ensures that most decisions are taken by the team as a whole.	☐	☐
8.	keeps their staff under control.	☐	☐
9.	is quick to praise another for their good performance.	☐	☐
10.	is quick to criticize others when they make mistakes.	☐	☐
11.	is trusting and trusted.	☐	☐
12.	prefers to be part of group creativity sessions rather than thinking creatively alone.	☐	☐
13.	provides emotional support to colleagues.	☐	☐
14.	is a coordinator rather than controller of their team.	☐	☐
15.	finds that if staff are told exactly what is required and why, they will agree to do it.	☐	☐
16.	prefers to work in a team rather than on their own.	☐	☐
17.	uses their authority to ensure that staff meet their targets.	☐	☐
18.	has well-developed listening skills and is a good listener.	☐	☐
19.	encourages individuals in the group to share their feelings and expectations.	☐	☐
20.	develops a caring and supportive environment.	☐	☐

21. believes that, when necessary, the judicious use of threats will get agreement. ☐ ☐

22. promotes not just their own ideas and suggestions but also those of colleagues. ☐ ☐

23. persuades individuals in the group to share information and support each other. ☐ ☐

24. persuades others with the use of their authority and appropriate rewards and punishments. ☐ ☐

25. provides regular feedback to their staff on their performance. ☐ ☐

26. likes to be in charge. ☐ ☐

27. helps others create a shared vision and understanding. ☐ ☐

28. prefers working with a team to working with an individual. ☐ ☐

29. recognizes the need to be sensitive to colleagues' feelings. ☐ ☐

30. disciplines poor performers. ☐ ☐

31. believes that the best agreement is when both sides win. ☐ ☐

32. pushes their own views strongly. ☐ ☐

33. usually carries out communication and feedback in a team context. ☐ ☐

34. makes staff aware what is said is meant, and that they should do what is requested. ☐ ☐

35. openly expresses their own thoughts and feelings, and encourages members of staff to express theirs. ☐ ☐

36. is a catalyst and facilitator rather than a commander of the group. ☐ ☐

Figure 2.2 *Inventory for a work colleague to record their perception of your leadership orientation*

Table 2.1 *Leadership orientation*

Controlling		Supporting		Team	
Self	*Other*	*Self*	*Other*	*Self*	*Other*
1	1	2	2	3	3
6	6	4	4	5	5
8	8	9	9	7	7
10	10	11	11	12	12
15	15	13	13	14	14
17	17	18	18	16	16
21	21	20	20	19	19
24	24	22	22	23	23
26	26	25	25	27	27
30	30	29	29	28	28
32	32	31	31	33	33
34	34	35	35	36	36

Total

Difference

'command and control'. If both scores are very high, whilst you have allowed your followers a certain amount of development, you have never learnt when to let go. The need to develop flexibility of style with individual followers and adapt your style according to given situations is covered under the heading, 'What is your leadership style?' on page 22.

Where there are perception gaps

Which is more relevant to leadership effectiveness – how we see ourselves or how others see us?

I think the latter. Of course, the direction of the gap is important. If you see yourself as moderate in the 'team' orientation and are seen as high, you are simply more effective than you thought yourself. It is important to accept the good news, because we get even better only if we explicitly recognize and develop a strength.

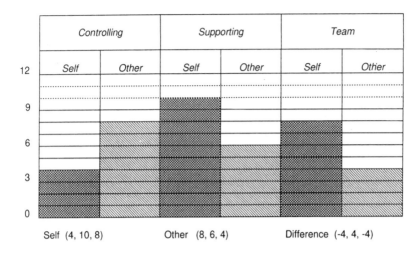

Figure 2.3 *An example of a completed scoring chart for the leadership orientation inventories*

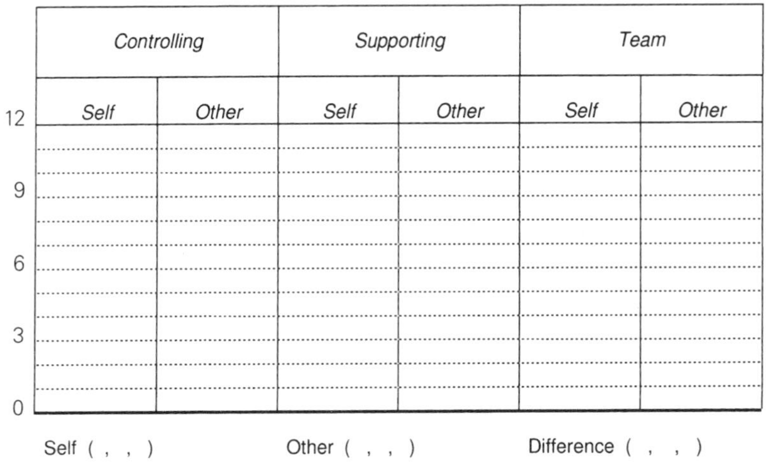

Figure 2.4 *A blank scoring sheet*

Conversely, if, as happens, we see ourselves as very strongly team-oriented and are not perceived as such, we need to look within the two sets of answers and identify the specific areas where there is disagreement. If it is a trusted colleague who completed the 'other' inventory, it would be worth exploring the specifics with them, as this will arm you with knowledge of what specific areas you need to be aware of and counter before you start building your team, if you have one.

The same holds for gaps in the other two orientations. Very weak perceived 'supporting' would be a cause for concern. The extreme of strongly perceived 'controlling' and low 'supporting' and 'team' suggest a leader who is permanently focused on managing tasks, not leading people and/or meeting their own needs to develop confidence and self-esteem.

How we can eliminate gaps in perception is covered in the next chapter.

WHAT IS YOUR LEADERSHIP STYLE?

Models of four leadership styles have been developed by a number of experts. I will use the one developed by Kenneth Blanchard, writer of the *One-minute Manager*.

The first thing you need to do is complete a chart to find out which of the four styles or style combinations you currently prefer and compare it with your colleague's perception of your style.

There then follows an explanation of each style, when it is appropriate to use which, as well as seeing how effective delegation can be seen as a progression of styles.

Completing the chart

I draw your attention to Figure 2.5, which shows a completed chart, using Charles' scores for 'Own perception' - 4, 10 (we ignore the 'team' score for this analysis) – and 'Another's perception' – 8, 6. We see that Charles sees himself as S3, and is seen as a combination of S2/S1. Please use Figure 2.6 to enter your own scores.

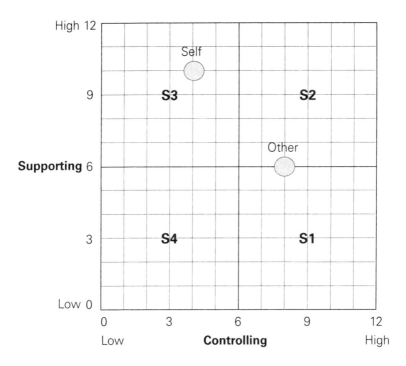

Figure 2.5 *Example of a completed leadership style chart*

Understanding each style

Let us look at each style in turn.

S1: Tell

There are three occasions when, as the leader, the 'tell' style should be used.

In a crisis. If there is a crisis, then it is the leader's role to resolve it. Imagine if the Captain of the *Titanic*, when the iceberg had struck, had called all his officers together and said, 'Gentlemen, we have a problem. We have just been struck by an iceberg. So let us pour ourselves a stiff drink, eh, and have a chin-wag – a

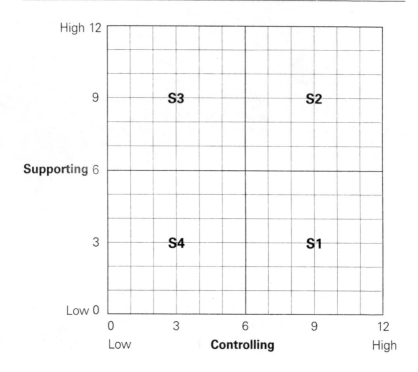

Figure 2.6 *A blank leadership style chart*

brainstorm to promote discovery of the various options, and then some time action planning, with, of course, a full review of the plan, before implementing it. It's 3 pm, and if we get started now, we should be ready for effective action in 4 hours.'

Of course he could not have done this! As leaders, in such a situation we seize control and tell our followers what to do, why and how so that the crisis is rapidly resolved.

I would emphasize that we do not simply tell people what to do, as some leaders do: we must also give a clear explanation of the crisis or the reason for the action we suggest. Nor is covering 'What?' and 'Why?' sufficient: we must give clear guidance on the specifics of the 'How?' For example, 'Gentlemen, we have been hit by an iceberg. We must abandon ship immediately with a minimum of panic. Harry, you will be responsible for managing the news to the passengers and organizing their move to the lifeboats; George, you will be responsible for getting the passengers into the lifeboats and lowering them to the sea, applying the principle of women and children first; Charles, you will send out distress signals; Matthew will... and so on. The sequence I propose is... Any questions, gentlemen? No? Then proceed to action.'

Follower new to role. Where a specific follower is new to a job, and likely to lack confidence and be feeling insecure, then we need to 'tell' in a constructive way – provide clear guidance on what needs to be done, why and how and monitor performance.

Sudden negative change. We will look at this in more detail in Chapter 10. However, sudden change, perceived negatively, can cause a loss of self-esteem, uncertainty and negative emotions. The leader needs to take control of the situation to avoid the team splitting at the seams or the individual becoming demotivated and incompetent.

S2: Coaching

This style is used where a follower has gained a degree of competence and confidence and while we will provide the 'What?' and 'Why?', we will also involve the follower in the 'How?', seek their input, and listen to the views expressed. So, there is a genuine dialogue on and agreement to the implementation.

S3: Supporting

This style is used when we have a confident and competent follower who can do the job well, but we remain in touch by having an 'open door' policy and being available to support if there are problems/unexpected difficulties encountered by our follower.

S4: Delegating

A style especially used at higher levels in an organization when the leader expects their lieutenants to be able to run the part of the organization for which they are responsible, and provides little direction or support.

Some key points

The progression through the four leadership styles can be viewed as an effective process towards delegation or empowerment. We should attempt this development path for all our followers, as then we are optimizing our own time – we can work less hard than we undoubtedly will if we remain locked into an S1 or S1/S2 combination, and we will be able to focus much more on the strategic aspects of our job.

If you refer back to the 16 actions suggested for effective leaders in Figure 1.2 (page 7), then the list by 'Develops the follower' can be seen as a progression from S1 to S4.

There is a need to avoid developing mind-sets or acting on false assumptions. A true story will serve to illustrate this. A senior associate in a law firm was seen as a star and destined for partnership. When talking to him, he said that the downside to this perception was that his partner never praised him for a job well done (S4 should be rare as a little bit of interest, support and praise goes a long, long way), occasionally delegated projects to him that were beyond his level of technical ability and failed to provide any coaching at all. He was being left to his own devices.

If we recognize the level of confidence and ability of our followers and the nature of the situation they face, we can then choose the leadership style that is appropriate. By doing this we develop a flexible and appropriate response.

Research on the collective views of leaders and their followers suggests that there is a significant gap in perception of leadership styles. Followers usually see us operating one level lower than we think we are ourselves. So, for instance, we may see ourselves operating with an S2/S3 combination, but we are seen as S1/S2.

This last point leads neatly on to the next chapter – all about gaps in perception and how to close them.

3

ELIMINATING PERCEPTION GAPS

In this chapter we provide a true story of the extent to which perception gaps can arise between a leader and a follower, consider how these gaps arise and, in the process, determine strategies for eliminating them.

THE TRUE STORY

In fact, this is two true stories rolled into one as the conversation with the bosses and one direct report of each of them were almost identical. In one instance, the boss was the Group Finance Director of a multinational travel services company (and the direct report was the Finance Director) and in the other the boss was a main Board director and Chief Executive Officer of a manufacturing subsidiary and the direct report was his Marketing Director.

First is the conversation with the boss, with Q standing for questioner and B for boss:

Q: 'So, how would you describe your leadership style?'
B: 'Well, I think I would say I was an empowering leader, who trusted his staff.'
Q: 'An empowering, trusting leader – very powerful. How do you demonstrate this leadership approach?'
B: 'Well, it's simple really. Let us say, a project crosses my desk that I have neither the time nor inclination to handle personally. I will call the appropriate person in, or, to be

honest, most of the time whoever is available as we are all so busy these days, and I say, "I trust you and I empower you. Here's this little project for you to do. I know you will do an excellent job – best of luck" or some such thing.'

'And what is more, usually a few days later, I have some spare time on my hands, so I pop along to help him with the project.'

Now to the follower's perspective:

Q: 'So, how you would describe the kind of leadership you receive?'

A: 'My boss is a dictator.' (The other follower used the word 'tyrant'.)

Q: 'Oh! dear. How does he demonstrate this dictatorial approach?'

A: 'Well, you know how overworked I am, with my increased responsibilities and number of direct reports? Well, in the midst of trying to cope, I get the dreaded summons to the boss' office. Then I hear the two words I hate most in the English language – "empower" and "trust". He waffles on about how he trusts me and is going to empower me, then dumps on me some God awful project, which I haven't time to do, and, sometimes, haven't got the technical skill to do. Then he dismisses me with words like "I know you'll do a good job".'

'Well, what do I do? I either dump it down , "Sorry – empower one of my staff!" or, more often than not, as my staff are working all hours like me, I try my best to do the job.'

'What is even worse is that a few days later, he saunters into my office, asks how I am getting on, reviews what I have done and points out all my mistakes!'

The bosses saw themselves as S3/S4 and were seen as S4 (dumping) and S1.

The existence of these perception gaps severely diminished the quality of the business relationships between these two bosses and their subordinates, as well as affecting the competence and stress levels of all. Both bosses had to spend more time checking (or, as they phrased it, 'supporting') than was necessary and the absence of coaching (for relevant projects) meant that mistakes were made and deadlines missed, which did not reflect well on the bosses in their superiors' eyes.

The followers had to work less effectively and efficiently than they could have done if they had received the proper coaching and support, which added to their stress levels. Additionally, they were seen as not sufficiently competent in the eyes of their bosses (despite the words uttered), which would affect their promotion prospects or, in these days of downsizing and/or organizational restructuring, prospects for continued employment.

HOW PERCEPTION GAPS ARISE

You will notice that in Figure 3.1 there are two gaps:

- ❑ *gap 1* the gap between conscious intent and manifestation
- ❑ *gap 2* the gap between manifestation and the impact on the other party – the follower.

We are here looking specifically at the relationship between leader and follower, but the gaps and their causes hold for any relationship, business or social. As an example, we will take a situation where we want to persuade a follower (let us call the follower Sally) to change the way she is managing a project.

Our conscious motivation or intent is to transfer a little of our expertise to the follower so that she does the project better. As we are the boss and accountable for the results of the project, there is an element of self-interest. We will also assume that Sally is the project leader and we hold only a watching brief. She has been given both the authority and responsibility to manage the project team. No gaps arise in the right environment with the right approach.

Let us say the words we use, with consistent non-verbal signals or body language, are, 'I have got a good idea as to how we can reduce the time taken to install the new network'.

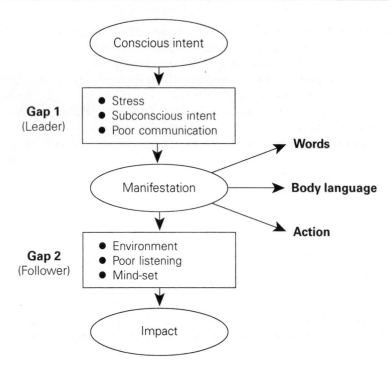

Figure 3.1 *How perception gaps arise*

Now:

❑ if this suggestion comes as part of a regular weekly review of the project with the follower
❑ there is an agenda and key aspects of the project are discussed
❑ (IT) is the item being discussed,

then, provided our idea is sound, it is likely to be gratefully accepted. There are no gaps. The suggestion is part and parcel of explicit expectations set and phrased in a positive, non-critical way. Because the behavioural manifestation expresses the intent effectively, there is no gap 1. When the environment is also right, there is no gap 2. We achieve our objective, which is to get the follower to 'change' – do something differently to how she would have done it without our effective intervention.

It is accepted because we have created an environment where there is a 'shared voyage of discovery'. The follower will be coming through with her ideas as well and both parties will be developing ideas together.

In the wrong environment, though, there is no gap 1, but we may cause a gap 2. We will return to this later in this chapter when we look at gap 2, but here we will focus on the causes of gap 1 and then how to eradicate them.

How the gap between intent and behavioural manifestation arises

Let us look at each cause in turn.

We are under stress

We may be under stress, feeling irritable, in a rush and so on, so we say to Sally 'The installation time for the new network can be reduced by 50 per cent. This is what you have to do…'. Interestingly, when under stress or in a rush, when we are feeling the pressure, there is a natural inclination to move into more of a 'tell' style or 'command and control' leadership approach. The problem with this is that some staff will only verbally agree and then ignore us afterwards and others will do their level best to implement our suggestions or 'instructions', but will not fully understand or 'own' the solution and so will implement them imperfectly.

In fact, we may well not bother with a face-to-face meeting, sending the follower an e-mail message or written note advising her of what she has to do to improve the management of her project. Putting yourself in your follower's shoes, would you see that intervention as a helpful suggestion, which acknowledges and respects your authority and competence as project leader? Neither would I, yet that was the intent!

Incidentally, there are many executives who use written instructions and e-mails as a matter of course, with no intention to upset or demotivate and no knowledge that that is the impact because the follower is not prepared to volunteer feedback – it is never requested. In any case, even if feedback were to be 'requested', it would never be honest. If the employee is on the way out, honest feedback may be volunteered and ignored! We look at promoting feedback in Chapter 6.

We are driven by the subconscious

A positive conscious intention may hide a subconscious or implicit intention that is more negative. So, our conscious desire may be to improve the position, but to build self-esteem we also want to criticize. The way we behave manifests such hidden intentions. For example, 'Sally, your plan to install the new network is flawed. I have come up with a way to reduce installation time by 50 per cent. This is what you have to do.'

Human nature being what it is, Sally is likely to pick the word flaw as the key word in the sentences and react negatively to what she perceives is implied criticism.

Incidentally, this cause is a very common one. I don't know if you have noticed, but often when two work colleagues get together to have a chat – or, for that matter, any two people do this in any setting – there can be a tendency to flatter each other and make the occasional unfavourable comment about anyone else not present whose name crops up! This combines positive and negative approaches to building self-esteem – building each other up and running others down to create a positive gap between ourselves and the other parties not present.

If we have low self-esteem as leaders, this negative manifestation of intent will be commonplace, though unrecognized, which is one reason for my suggesting that we should develop our feelings of competence and confidence as a precursor to effective leadership.

We communicate badly

The third gap is simply poor communication. If we are the expert and know more than the follower on IT matters (perhaps one of her team is the IT expert), then we may use language, jargon or concepts she does not fully understand. She may perceive us as blinding them with science or proving our superiority in the chosen area, none of these manifestations being intended. Unless the follower acknowledges her lack of understanding and seeks and receives clarification (and often people are reluctant to expose their ignorance), then implementation of the change will not be fully effective or the wrong change will be implemented – neither of which is a desirable outcome.

In summary, if their is a gap 1, the manifestation of intent will produce an impact unavoidably different to the intent. The other person accurately responds to the behaviour manifested, as that is the explicit demonstration of intent. They will assume, because of the gap, an intent that is consistent with the manifestation, but which is not the initiator's actual intent. Hence the misperception, which can be so damaging to relationships and to the effective initiation of change. In this case there is no gap 2.

How to close the gap

Looking at each cause in turn, we need to do the following.

❑ *Recognize and try to eliminate stress, at least temporarily.* Avoid the hasty memo or sudden intervention by telephone or 'dropping in'. In fact, as already suggested, what will help significantly, both in terms of our stress and that of our followers, is if we have a policy of proactively managing the environment so that it is conducive to the acceptance of our suggestion before we make our intentions known. However, we may not be in a position to hold regular meetings as our followers are geographically dispersed or the dictates of deadlines mean that we cannot wait. In such cases, it is better to telephone than send an e-mail.

❑ *Deliberately use the 'assertive pause'.* This involves pausing to breathe at least twice as slowly as normal, thereby carrying oxygen-rich blood to our brains and literally 'clearing our heads'. This will enable us to consciously consider our intention and motivations and try to identify and eliminate any critical aspects *before* we speak.

❏ *Try to avoid jargon.* As a matter of policy, check that the other party has understood what they have agreed to.

How the gap between manifestation and impact arises

While manifestation of intent can be totally consistent with the intent, the environment in which the interchange occurs, or the poor listening skills of the receiver or their mind-set towards the transmitter, means that the actual impact is different to the intent/manifestation. Let us look at each of these elements in turn.

The leader enters the wrong environment

As already mentioned, the environment in which an interchange takes place is critical to the outcome. So, if the message is delivered in a way that is consistent as to intention and manifestation, then the impact can still be negative because the environment is wrong.

Both the leader and the follower have a responsibility to pro-actively manage the environment. As suggested, the leader should avoid the unexpected, such as dropping by or telephoning with their new idea. The follower also needs to be assertive when the leader is entering the wrong environment, advising them that they are rushed off their feet, busy in a meeting, going to a meeting and so on.

The follower does not listen

Say the follower does not pick up the message correctly. There can be a cause and effect relationship with the environment – the listener is distracted by pressure of other work, or the listener has failed to listen actively, only focusing on part of the message or picking up the wrong end of the stick.

Such events are no problem for the leader, provided they do not make assumptions that agreement means understanding, and ensure that any assumptions are checked. We can see that, although in theory leaders can be considered as not being responsible for the causes of gap 2, they need to be proactive to avoid harmful effects that result. It is the price paid for being the leader.

The follower has a fixed mind-set

People will often not believe the evidence of their own eyes. It happens in personal relationships and in business relationships. People come to expect what happened in the past to continue and pass judgements that become unwritten rules of behaviour towards the other person in the relationship. They do not notice changes in attitude or approach. So, if the followers perceive the initiator of change, their leader, as someone who has in the past criticized them when they suggested change or told them what to do out of stress or communicated poorly (that is, there has always been a gap 1), they may well react to effective communication of intent as if there was still a gap!

This is a very difficult situation for leaders. They are likely to think, 'Here am I, trying to respect the follower's position as project leader and suggesting a useful change in a positive way, and all she does is throw it back in my face. Well, I am not standing for that. Now, let me tell you...'.

You may discover a direct way of handling this situation. All I can suggest is an avoidance strategy – the generic solution we considered at the beginning. If you, as leader, ensure that the environment is right, that itself will begin to change the perceptions of the person with the negative mind-set.

Finally, we need to consider the cumulator.

What is the cumulator?

The cumulator is a combination of a cause or causes in both gap 1 and gap 2. They combine in an explosive way, leading to the most unfavourable outcomes, from a shouting match to employee dismissal. For instance, a leader's conscious intention is to make a helpful intervention, but he criticizes, and the intervention occurs in the wrong environment, in front of the follower's own subordinates. This is not deliberate on the part of the initiator – the leader has just rushed in with his brainwave.

Problems like these will be eliminated by adopting the generic solution – regular, planned review meetings. What is also required is disciplining oneself to recognize that, in all but the most exceptional cases, there is no need to 'act in haste and repent at leisure'.

It is vital that such perception gaps are reduced, if not eliminated, as they act – as the original story demonstrated – as a considerable demotivator.

Motivating staff is one of the core responsibilities of an effective leader, and the subject of the next chapter.

4

MOTIVATING STAFF

The extent to which we are motivated or demotivated in the workplace will determine how well we perform. In this chapter, we look at what motivates you, then fit that into relevant models of motivation and conclude by considering what the key strategies are that leaders should adopt to motivate their staff – linking these back to what effective leaders do.

WHAT MOTIVATES YOU IN THE WORKPLACE?

Consider the following job characteristics and their definitions:

- ❑ *high pay:* receiving a salary that will enable you to improve your existing standard of living;
- ❑ *development:* the opportunity to improve yourself by learning new skills and taking on more demanding work;
- ❑ *friendly environment:* working with people (including subordinates and superiors) who are friendly and approachable;
- ❑ *autonomy:* being able to set your own objectives, to plan your working day and have control over how you do your own job;
- ❑ *security:* the assurance of continued employment and a comfortable retirement;
- ❑ *responsibility:* the opportunity to make decisions, be accountable for the results and have control over some (or all) of the organizations' resources, such as people, money, materials;

❑ *status:* recognition from others in some non-monetary tangible form of the importance of your position in the organization, such as having a secretary, an office, access to 'upper echelon' dining facilities;
❑ *achievement:* the opportunity to solve problems and be able to see the results of your efforts.

Now list three characteristics that are of the greatest importance to you in a job.

You may well ask, 'So what?', but what emerges (from the replies of many managers to this request to rank the characteristics) are two key factors:

❑ the priorities vary enormously from person to person. There is no single 'motivator' (I put the word in quotes for a reason that will become clear in the next section). Leaders cannot rely on one right answer.
❑ the list changes for a given manager over time. For instance, post recession in the UK, security moved up significantly!

To explain why this list was selected, why not all of these job characteristics are 'motivators' and why the list can vary not only from individual to individual, but for the same individual over time, we shall now look at Maslow's hierarchy of needs. Maslow was an eminent psychologist.

WHAT DO WE NEED?

Maslow's hierarchy of needs is shown in Figure 4.1.

The key points in relation to this hierarchy are that:

❑ until lower-level needs are fulfilled, we do not progress to satisfying higher-level needs;
❑ the hierarchy can be seen as a psychological path to maturity – Maslow suggests that any leader has the moral responsibility to help each follower to reach and fulfil higher-level needs;

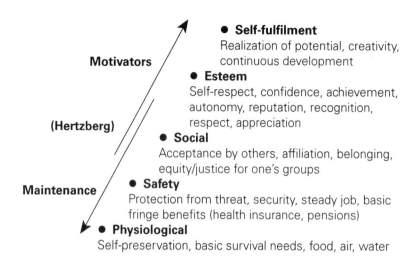

Figure 4.1 *Maslow's hierarchy of needs*

❑ where we are on the hierarchy will be a measure of our self-esteem and confidence, which, again, is why it is so important for us as leaders to develop self-awareness and confidence – we are ineffective leaders if we are locked into low levels of self-esteem;

❑ shocks to the system – that is, fundamental changes in our working (and other) environment – can send us tumbling down, both individually and collectively, as evidenced when civil war broke out in Bosnia;

❑ we need to differentiate between lower-level needs and higher-level needs.

You will notice on the left in Figure 4.1 there is an arrow pointing upwards marked 'motivators' and an arrow pointing downwards marked 'maintenance' factors. This is a development of Maslow's model by Herzberg, who called them 'hygiene factors'. They are also referred to as 'dissatisfiers'. Let us take some examples to explain the difference between them.

Assume that we enjoy an excellent in-house restaurant, which is provided to us for no charge. This satisfies a basic need. Assume also that the powers that be decide to add two more courses to the menu. This is good news, but will not result in us dashing back to our office to put in that extra hour. Meeting a basic need does not motivate us. Similarly, if we feel totally secure in our jobs, while we may be driven by fear (not an effective motivator) to gain that security, we will not be motivated to work harder once we feel secure.

However, an announcement that the restaurant is going to be closed as part of a cost-cutting exercise will cause extreme dissatisfaction. Until we can come to terms with this removal of a basic need (see Chapter 10), then we will be distracted from focusing on higher-level needs – the things that actually motivate us.

In considering the implications of these ideas for organizations and leaders, see Figure 4.2. The outer circle consists of characteristics that define the context in which the actual job takes place, while the inner circle consist of the characteristics of the job itself. The former consists of hygiene factors and the latter of true motivators. You will notice that the eight characteristics we introduced at the beginning consisted of those hygiene factors where the leader had an element of control, as well as motivators.

Before proceeding, I have one caveat I would like to note in relation to Herzberg's model. Interpersonal relations are considered by Herzberg to be a hygiene factor. He was carrying out his research some decades ago in the US. Interpersonal relationships are deemed to be of much higher importance in the East. Indeed, these days in the West, the importance of effective communication internally and externally – the need for cultures to consist of internal behaviours that reflect external behaviours so that customers can be delighted – is recognized as being vital to success.

Both Herzberg and, to a lesser extent, Maslow were prisoners of the present they researched. Interpersonal relationships (the ability to communicate effectively with other human beings) rank alongside achievement, responsibility and so on as motivators. That is also the view of such culture experts as Roger Harrison.

Before looking at the key motivational strategies, relevant points to make here are as follows:

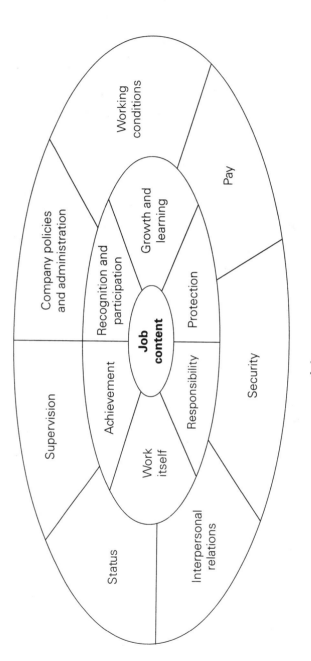

Figure 4.2 *Herzberg's motivation at work*

❑ All the four action areas for an effective leader (set out in Figure 1.2, page 7) and the actions that flow from them are motivators, providing the timing is right. Putting work into its context is fundamental, particularly the need to provide vision and targets. As someone once said, 'You cannot aim the rifle if you have not got a target'. If we have a picture of an exciting future, we are automatically moving towards fulfilling the highest-level need. Having clear, agreed, shorter-term goals and targets provides the route map along the way.

'Developing the follower' – using the S1 to S4 leadership styles in progression – enables us as leaders to move our followers along the psychological path to maturity.

'Leading by example' is necessary to ensure that our followers believe what we say as they see consistency of action to match the fine leadership words. Additionally 'people buy people not products' and so effective leaders become beacons of light in the darkness.

Finally, 'Providing support' – demonstrating how valuable we see our followers, using the carrot of praise rather than the stick of criticism – helps build their self-esteem.

❑ The differences between hygiene factors were never recognized during decades of industrial strife and are not sufficiently recognized today. In the past, and some parts of the present, trade unions focus on pay and terms and conditions. This is because managers fail to provide true motivators. In their absence, the focus of attention becomes dissatisfiers. Of course, with growing work insecurities, the increasing use of individual (and not team) targets, the carrot of more money and the stick of redundancy, employees turn their attention to dissatisfiers – such as 'How much money can I make?' and 'What is my status in this organization?' Yet, many years ago, I came across a large company where the workplace was team-based – a stimulating, challenging and fun environment. Competitors would seek to tempt the stars away with financial offers of more than a third above current packages – to no avail.

THE KEY MOTIVATIONAL STRATEGIES

The following are what followers say are the most motivating strategies leaders should adopt: When I looked again at the list, I realized that, almost without exception, the strategies were absent or very weak in most current cultures. We are thus seeking motivation where it is lacking.

Promote effective feedback

Feedback is not generally promoted. It certainly is not promoted by the annual downwards appraisal, which both parties tend to dread and so defer for as long as possible. In these appraisals, leaders tell followers where they are weak (S1 domination), or where they are strong and weak (S2), or they praise and say the followers are brilliant (to avoid a demotivated backlash) (S3), or just accept whatever the follower says (S4).

The key to effective feedback lies in the skill of 'promoting discovery', covered in the next chapter, and its use in feedback situations, covered in Chapter 8.

Receiving effective feedback is highly motivating as it provides certainty where there was doubt, acknowledges the strengths (including those we may not have fully appreciated) we are demonstrating that are relevant to the job we undertake and ensures we have an action plan (usually involving both parties) to develop and grow so that we do our job better, have a greater sense of achievement and can walk along the path to more challenging and stimulating work.

Provide supportive leadership/adapt your leadership styles

Providing supportive leadership arises from an excess of S1. As leaders, we often think – mostly unconsciously – that this is the heart of what leadership is all about.

Followers mention adapting your leadership styles because of the general inflexibility of leadership styles they see around them. Leaders become comfortable with a given style or style combination.

Delegate

I think it is ironic that so many leaders are stressed out of their minds because they won't delegate. Reasons are:

❑   perceived lack of time;
❑   belief that they are the most competent to do the job;
❑   lack of faith in the follower;
❑   fear that if they delegate away their jobs, they will have no jobs to keep.

Followers, however, are crying out for more challenging and stimulating work so that they can take on more responsibility, achieve more, develop and grow.

If leaders recognize that any follower has the potential to improve, and that effective delegation is a process that needs to be planned – not a simple act of dumping – then stress would reduce significantly for all parties involved.

Equally, if you are successful, you will be praised for running such a splendid ship and be able to make a greater contribution to the strategic end of your role.

Allow risk-taking

Taking risks is a prerequisite to learning, and learning is necessary in a world of change – change being defined here as 'making or becoming different'. Many leaders blame when mistakes are made and discourage risk-taking.

The key to success is to manage risks. By means of effective coaching and review processes, what risks can be taken can be agreed and parameters set, avoiding the consequences of just letting go (S4) or keeping total control (S1).

Train and develop

While many organizations are introducing formal training and development programmes and personal development plans as the back-end of the appraisal process, many are not. Moreover, the training and development process has to be effective. We in the training world use the jargon 'user chooser'.

Where the employee determines and chooses what training they have, the process is much more effective than when they are sent for 'remedial therapy' or where the development plans have been told or sold, but not discovered. Additionally, many training establishments rely too heavily on lecturing, not knowing that is not the way we learn. Indeed, research carried out by the UK Post Office and IBM (UK) proves that if we are lectured at, we remember 70 per cent after three days and a miserly 10 per cent after three months (and after a few years, I would suggest hardly anything at all).

However, if input is supported by explanation, then we are tested (preferably in small, effective study groups) and then there is a shared review of the results/experience to produce short cuts or new knowledge, our memory after three days soars above 85 per cent and after three months is above 65 per cent.

Generate high expectations

In one company, once, the CEO decided that the staff should set their own targets, and not have them mandated or set for them. The managers were very dubious about this (but, of course, had to go along with it) as they assumed the employees would be lazy – setting themselves low, easily achievable targets. Much to their surprise, they found the reverse happened and they had to try and persuade their staff to reduce their targets, which they felt were so high, they would not be achieved, which would demotivate the staff.

Provide goals

As noted earlier, 'You cannot aim a rifle, if you have no target.'

Acknowledge achievement

A single word of praise has more motivational power than a thousand words of blame.

Having looked at what motivates, we next turn to the key skills necessary to implement some of these strategies effectively, skills that help us to become more effective leaders.

5

QUESTIONING EFFECTIVELY

In this chapter, we look at the core skill of effective questioning. First of all we provide examples of ineffective and effective questioning, then analyse to determine what the right questions are and conclude the chapter by looking at what to do to become an effective questioner – developing our followers and improving our relationships with them.

ASKING THE RIGHT QUESTIONS

First, let us look at one example of ineffective questioning, then two examples of effective questioning.

Questioning ineffectively

We eavesdrop on a conversation between a boss (B) and a subordinate (S) that may have met the boss' objectives, but completely demotivated the employee.

B: 'Chris tells me that you were late again this morning. Is that correct?'
S: 'Yes. I'm very sorry.'
B: 'In fact, you were half an hour late. Am I right?'
S: 'Yes.' (mumbled)
B: 'To be completely accurate (and you know that I like to have my facts right), you have been half an hour late every day this week, have you not?'

S: 'Yes.'
B: 'Well, this firm does not tolerate laziness and tardiness. I am a fair person, as you know, but I don't beat about the bush. If this occurs once more, we will start the disciplinary procedures against you. Do I make myself clear?'
S: 'Yes.'
B: 'Well, don't let it happen again.'

Questioning effectively

First of all, let us have a re-run of the conversation, but this time with a boss who has learnt what the right questions are and how to ask them. Then we shall look at how a problem was avoided by asking the right questions in the right sequence.

Communicating effectively

B: 'Chris tells me that you were half an hour late this morning, and, in fact, every morning this week. Is that correct?'
S: 'Yes. I'm very sorry.'
B: 'Tell me why were you late?'
S: 'Well, the traffic's been very bad.'
B: 'But the traffic's always bad, and you normally come to work on time. So, what's the problem?'
S: 'Well... My mother's very poorly.'
B: 'I'm sorry to hear that, John. It must be very tough for you – I know you are very close to your mother.'
S: 'Yes, Alex, it's tough all right.'
B: (Pause) 'But, I don't see why you have been getting here late, John.'
S: 'Well, mother now needs our full-time care. She can't be left on her own for a minute. Barbara, my wife, works nights and doesn't get back home until half-past eight. I immediately set off for work, but, because of the traffic, I'm late.'
B: 'I see. And because you want to get home as soon as possible to relieve Barbara, who must be tired out, you have left work at the normal time, rather than making the time up?'

S: 'Yes and no, Alex. I have left at the normal time, but I have cut my lunch break to half an hour, and made up the time that way.'
B: 'I see. I've no problem with that at all.'

Solving a problem

This is a true story. The Alaskan Electricity Company faced terrible problems a number of years ago. It managed over 1000 miles of overground telegraph poles, supplying electricity to a sparse and widely scattered population in very hostile weather conditions. As a result of the terrible weather, ice and snow gathered on the overhead cables, which frequently snapped under the weight. Teams of men had to travel very long distances to repair these cables. The costs of such operations exhausted all the profits.

The company solved the problem by a group of people questioning effectively. These are the questions that were asked.

'Why don't we shake the poles?'
'That would be difficult with over 1000 miles of poles – but let's develop the theme.'
'OK. Why don't we get bears to shake the poles?'
'Well, yes... but how can we persuade the bears to shake the poles? How can we motivate the bears?'
'Well, why don't we put meat on top of the poles? In their attempts to reach the top of the poles to eat the meat, they will shake the poles and dislodge the ice and snow.'
'But how do we get meat to the top of the poles?'
'I know, why don't we use helicopters to fly the meat to the poles and place it on top for the bears?'
'I have a better idea. Why don't we use the helicopters to remove the ice and snow with their whirring blades and forget about all the bears?'

And that is what the Alaskan Electricity Company did – with considerable cost saving.

ANALYSING THE CONVERSATIONS

Now, let's look back at the conversations and problem and consider the differences between ineffective and effective questioning.

The key difference is the use of 'open' questions as opposed to 'closed' questions. As Rudyard Kipling wrote:

I kept six honest serving men.
They taught me all I knew;
Their names were what and why and when,
And how and where and who.

The types of and differences between open and closed questions are set out in Figure 5.1.

We all, with the rare exception, have a tendency to ask closed questions. There are three key reasons for this:

❑ education;
❑ psychology;
❑ ignorance.

Education

Our schooling is much more about finding answers – being provided with information that we use to develop conclusions – than it is about promoting discovery. As a result, we have an inevitable bias towards asking questions that provide answers.

Psychology

One great advantage of closed questions is that there are immediate answers. We know subconsciously that by asking a closed question, we are guaranteeing that we will have an answer. This means that outcomes are certain and controlled. Most of us like to be in control and even if we don't, we like a degree of certainty.

With open questions, there is an unpredictability of outcomes, generating uncertainty and the possibility that we could lose control of the conversation. However, this is what we perceive,

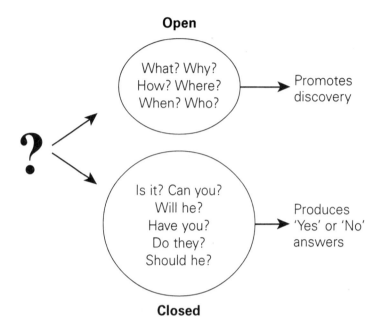

Figure 5.1 *Open and closed questions*

not the reality. An effective questioner and listener will be able to control both the direction and flow of any conversation.

Ignorance

As we have seen, few of us are taught about open questions.

With the ineffective conversation, there were only closed questions. With the effective conversation, there were three open and two closed.

With the problem, there were only open questions – eight in all.

WHAT TO DO TO QUESTION EFFECTIVELY

Here we look at key actions to take to ensure that we have an effective conversation with a follower. The context could be development, appraisal or problem-solving. The approaches are based on the desire to get the follower to think for themselves, to discover where they are strong or weak, rather than the traditional 'product' push – us telling followers what their strengths and weaknesses are, or solving the problem for them.

Note that the techniques and approaches described are just as relevant in any other relationship, such as that with a customer or partner.

Think first

With the time and place known in advance, the more we think and plan the conversation, the more effective it will be. Additionally, during the meeting, using the 'assertive pause' – pausing and breathing more slowly and deeply than normal to clear our heads and control negative emotions – ensures that we remain in control of ourselves and, hence, the questions we ask.

Think open question

I was facilitating a practical session to help develop effective questioning skills in some managers from one of our clients that involved the following activities. One manager comes up with a real problem or issue they want to discuss, another asks open questions in order to fully understand the problem, with two others and myself in an observer role during the questioning and then providing feedback. In one case, the questioner asked 1 open question, followed by 14 closed, and ended up pushing a solution to a problem he did not understand, much to the dissatisfaction of his 'client'.

While this last case is an extreme, the general norm, as we have established, is that we find it difficult to ask the right question, and so we must consciously think of the right open question to ask. For instance, when recapping, we should not summarize and then ask the closed question 'Am I right?', but rather, 'What have I omitted?' In the former case, the follower will simply say, 'Yes, you are.' In the latter, they will be much more inclined to advise the speaker of an omission.

This open approach is equally important with a team. If we brief a team about a task and then ask 'Have you all understood?', invariably, they will say 'Yes', thinking 'I don't want to look silly or inattentive in front of the boss'. However, if we ask someone to summarize – 'Now, Jane, just to ensure we are all clear, what do you think is our objective?' – this will lead to knowledge of where there are gaps, and, by checking with each group member, ensure everyone is singing from the same hymnsheet. This is better than a cacophony of sound emanating during the implementation phase, which, rather late in the day, forces us to realize that our assumption of understanding generated from the closed question approach was invalid.

Additionally, when establishing facts, rather than stating the facts and asking 'Do you agree?', it is much better to go the open route. For example, saying 'What are the facts?', and, when all the evidence has been brought into play, continue with, 'And let us think of any information we may have overlooked' before getting the closed agreement.

Avoid leading questions

Leading questions can be phrased in a closed or open style. They are the antithesis of promoting discovery or even problem-solving as they push or lead to the 'one right answer'. For example, 'The Chairman thinks we should sack Jones. What do you think?' and 'Surely you don't have any doubts about our new mission do you?'

A variation of this is the 'loaded' question. With a leading question, our own views are implicit. In a loaded question, they are explicit or loaded in. Here are some examples:

❑ 'Do you not agree that John has poor time-keeping?'
❑ 'Why don't you drop dead?!'

Not very open questions!

Avoid 'logical' closed alternatives

Let us say the issue under discussion is a drop in sales: 'Well, clearly we have to either reduce costs or increase revenue. Which do you favour?'

Far, far better to go the open route: 'Let us consider all the options we could take to reverse this trend'. Incidentally, 'or' can be used exclusively, as in the above case (although there is no reason for not doing both) or conjunctively, that is, both alternatives can be selected. So, the following kind of question should be avoided.

Q: 'Did you go to the cinema or the theatre?'
A: 'Yes!'

Use perceptive, probing questions

A perceptive, probing question is one that you can only ask when you have become a good listener.

When you ask good open questions, the other person opens up – that is their purpose. In the course of answering the particular question, they almost invariably drop in a phrase or even a sentence that is significant. This is inevitable as you are getting them to think, so either they reveal what was hidden from you or reveal what was latent or subconscious (hidden from them) and/or come up with completely new thoughts.

If you are listening acutely, you can easily pick up this significant phrase as there will usually be a slight change in the tone of voice or even body language.

Let us take the example of the manager, who asked 1 open, followed by 14 closed questions of the 'problem holder'. The problem as originally stated was that the 'problem holder' was a leader of a number of teams, each of which had a team leader, one of whom had resigned. He had complete autonomy as to what actions he took, and he had to decide whether to hire in a new team leader, promote from within the existing team (downsizing) or promote from within and hire a new team member.

First of all, he overstressed the word 'autonomy'. No one in business has complete autonomy these days, and he had a boss, who would have some views that he needed to ascertain, but that was not brought up.

Next, although the questioner asked all these closed questions, the 'problem holder' responded as if they were open because he was so anxious to air this real, important, work-related problem. On three occasions he dropped these little clues, but the matter was left unprobed.

On the first occasion, he referred, during a series of statements, to the fact that he would have a 'bigger job', and this should have been picked up on and probed. Something along the lines of the following.

Q: 'That's interesting. I noticed you mentioned that you would be taking on a bigger job. In what ways will your job become bigger?'

On the second occasion, he dropped in the phrase 'moving away', which should have led to three open questions:

Q1, 2 and 3: 'Thanks for that. You mentioned that you would be moving away. Where will you be going?' After the reply: 'When will you be going?' and, after that reply: 'And what will be the impact on your teams?'

Funnily enough, the third occasion was the *cri de coeur*. The 'problem holder' referred in the midst of other issues and points to 'how he could keep his staff motivated'.

The real problem, subsequently uncovered as a result of effective questioning, was: 'How do I keep my teams motivated, when I am going to take on additional responsibilities and be physically separate from them?'

Use the right wording

The way the question is worded will have a major impact on the answer given. The general rule is to focus the question so as to focus the other person. Some examples are:

❑ 'What do you mean precisely?' is better than 'What do you mean?', which could lead to 'I mean what I say.'
❑ 'In what ways is the job bigger?' is better than 'How much bigger is the job?', which could lead to the answer 'much, much bigger!'
❑ 'What are all the possible actions we can take to reduce absenteeism' is better than 'How do we reduce absenteeism?', or 'What could all the possible reasons be for sales falling' rather than 'Why have sales fallen?' Both the former increase the probability of a wider spectrum of ideas.

Keep questions simple

On a video, we have a persuasion role play involving two managers where one took more than ten minutes to ask his question. You should have seen the body language of the listener! If we are not confident or we are too involved or we are too rushed and speak before we think, we can get lost. We can start a question, go on a gentle ramble or lecture tour, recover and revert back to the question in hand. This is to be avoided, of course, as it makes us look silly and puts the listener to sleep! We must keep our questions simple and to the point.

Keep questions single

A golden rule of effective questioning is 'one at a time'. More than one question can lead to confusion or evasion. The respondent can select which one to answer, and the other one or ones can be lost in the subsequent discussion.

A classic example of this occurred a few years ago, when a back-bench Labour MP put forward written questions, intended to embarrass the government by showing the extent of sex discrimination in the Civil Service. Not only did he ask multiple questions, but ended by asking whether male staff or female staff were in the majority!

The junior minister's written reply to the entire set of questions was one word – 'Yes'!

Provide answers, when asked

There can be a danger that we get into an exclusive open question mind-set and so always end up answering a question with a question! Sharing your experiences and giving your opinions is a vital part of a leadership role. As we know, followers can lack confidence and need guidance and support. The trick is to try to build up confidence, promote discovery, develop thinking – shift the problem monkey back onto the shoulders where it should rightly rest – by asking all the right open questions. However, if and when you are asked for your opinion or your experience, then give it freely. The point is not to impose it early on, but to pull first and push later (if asked).

Too often, we simply push with all those closed, leading, logical alternative questions, and there is no real dialogue, no discovery and relationship enhancement.

Practise

As we have seen, being an effective questioner (and listener) does not come naturally to most. Thus the only way you will improve is to practise, practise, practise, practise and then practise again.

Now, having considered effective questioning in some depth, let us turn to the other side of the coin – active listening – in the next chapter.

6

LISTENING ACTIVELY

Unless we can listen effectively or actively to our followers, then we will throw all our good questions down the drain, along with the relationship. In this chapter, we answer three questions.

❑   Why is listening difficult?
❑   How can we identify poor listening?
❑   How can we become better listeners?

WHY IS LISTENING DIFFICULT?

There are six reasons for this.

Talkers are rewarded

Most of us learnt as babies that making a noise brought us attention. As children, the noisiest and loudest often became the leaders and innovators of childhood games and activities. In formal education, those children who always answered questions and spoke clearly and distinctly were more favoured and praised. And in adult and business life, this pattern continues. Those who make the most noise often gain more attention than they or their opinions deserve.

In the example of the boss and subordinate's ineffective conversation, the boss was a talker. He loved the sound of his own voice and only asked closed questions.

We are more important

Sometimes we say to ourselves – though rarely at the conscious level – that we are more important than the follower to whom we are talking. This is understandable as we all need to build our self-esteem and one way to do this is to feel superior to the individual with whom we are conversing. This reality can be reinforced given our 'superior' status. If we think we are more important – consciously or not – we will not listen actively.

We are more knowledgeable

A little knowledge is a dangerous thing. A lot of knowledge can be even more dangerous when it comes to listening. It is a variation on the perception of importance reason, but this time it is not a perception that the follower to whom we are talking is not important, but that what they may have to say – the content – is not important. We know more than them, and say to ourselves, deep down, 'Those who know nothing, have nothing to say'. Innocence and ignorance can be the source of much creativity and subsequent knowledge. Many inventions have come into being because somebody did not know 'it couldn't be done' or did not accept 'this is the way we do things round here' and somebody else listened.

However, most of us succumb individually and collectively to the 'new boy syndrome'. 'Until you have earned your spurs, proved your competence, you have nothing to say'.

We think faster than the follower speaks

This means that we have time available that can be put to good use, by concentrating and trying to fully comprehend what is being said to us; or to bad use, by allowing distractions and our own thoughts to intrude.

Our mind-sets

From the moment of our birth, we enter an uncertain world that has a complexity and a dynamic we can never comprehend. We are therefore driven, whether consciously or not, to manage that uncertainty. Some of us are capable of tolerating, even enjoying, high levels of ambiguity and uncertainty, but for all of us there is a degree and intensity to it that is unbearable.

To enable us to cope, we create and confirm areas of certainty – beliefs, assumptions, attitudes and opinions that we do not consciously question. If we did, we would raise the level of uncertainty in our lives. We would be taking a risk as we do not know what is the breaking point for us.

The stronger our mind-sets – which are likely to become stronger still in this age of increasing uncertainty – the more we can only listen to ourselves. We need to carry out a conscious and deliberate act of control and commit to change before we can ask the right question and listen effectively to the answers.

We can be poor speakers

The fault does not always lie with the listener; we can be poor speakers. We can speak too quickly. We can send out too much information. We can send out veiled messages with unsuitable speech patterns or mixed messages by using body language that is inconsistent with the words we speak.

The follower makes it difficult for us.

A key skill of an effective questioner is to use the power of questions to ensure that the messages received are clear to us and, in the process, clarify them for the follower!

HOW CAN WE IDENTIFY POOR LISTENING?

If we can identify poor listening in ourselves, we can improve. If we identify poor listening in the follower, we can rectify the situation. Not only should we listen effectively to the follower, but ensure the messages we transmit are effectively picked up. Again, this can be achieved by using simple questions to ensure comprehension.

At the heart of poor listening is body language – the non-verbal signals transmitted in the form of the gestures we make or postures we adopt. However, language also has a part to play. There are six useful classifications.

Aggressive listening

There are two types:

❑ deliberate;
❑ accidental.

Deliberate

We don't want to listen, but we have been forced to listen because of, say, a direct, emotional request. We have responded aggressively. Our heart is not in it, and we feel resentful. We fold our arms, presenting a barrier to the receipt of information, our posture is stiff and we tend to glare.

The only way to avoid deliberate, aggressive listening is not to be aggressive! On a more practical level, we can deploy the 'assertive pause'. If we receive a request we did not anticipate, we are automatically likely to respond emotionally. If we don't like the request, the emotions will be negative and, in this case of a direct request, we will fall into aggressive listening.

By using the assertive pause, we will think more clearly, control the immediate negative emotional reaction and respond with effective questions and active listening.

Accidental

We feel we ought to be listening, we want to listen, but are not very skilled at 'active listening' and try too hard. We feel the need to reassure the follower verbally with a 'Yes, I am listening to you!', which is a give-away to the follower that we are not! Our concentration at the conscious level makes us lean forward (perhaps invading the follower's body space unintentionally) with a stiff posture. This results in what we think is an interesting look being perceived as a discomforting stare!

The only way to avoid this type of aggressive listening – because it is not conscious – is to practise active listening.

Passive listening

A very common form of poor listening! This is when we have no desire to speak, have resigned ourselves to listen (perhaps the follower likes to hear the sound of their own voice) and we drift off, slumped in the chair, body half turned away from the speaker, hand over mouth to conceal the occasional yawn, and little eye contact as we tend to look elsewhere. If we catch ourselves out in this mode, we need to ask a probing, open question – interrupt. 'That's an interesting point, but how does it relate to the issue we are focusing on?'

Listening interruptus

This is when we don't want to listen, we want to speak. In the early stages, assuming we cannot find an appropriate moment to interrupt, we are likely to fidget in some fashion, such as drumming our fingers or playing with a pencil (assuming that is not the way we display nerves). Then we lean forward and interrupt.

Often, both parties can be in this mode simultaneously. The result is a bewildering dance of never-completed statements or themes, as the talking prize is snatched one from the other, then back again. The bodies move forward when talking and back as the threatened invasion of personal body space forces the involuntary move. The occasional fidget manifests itself if the unnatural state of silence is too prolonged!

The only way to avoid this is by developing the right mind-set or attitude in advance of the conversation, and the questioning skill to close down the verbiage of the follower.

Logical listening

This is when we listen with our minds, not our hearts. We are deaf to the messages conveyed by the way the follower speaks the words and the non-verbal signals. We hear and respond to the words only. 'I'm getting divorced' receives the reply 'Then get a lawyer'.

Logical listening is often the precursor to passive listening. We start off a little detached because we are only operating at the logical and not emotional level. We are quick with the obvious logical solutions, then become bored and lapse into passive listening.

Logical listening can also be the precursor to aggressive listening. Followers want to share the feelings behind the verbal messages they make, and are quite capable of working out the logical responses for themselves. They pick up the lack of eye contact and the lack of warm, supportive body language, which compounds their sense of irritation stemming from the statement of the obvious. Assuming the conversation has not been terminated, they will often make the emotional appeal: 'You are just not listening to me.'

We will then have the direct, emotional response (perceived negatively) that can trigger aggressive listening in the absence of that assertive pause.

Arrogant listening

When we feel very comfortable and confident, often in front of a subordinate, we can adopt an 'aggressive' posture – hands clasped behind our heads, leaning back, legs stretched forwards or even on a desk (at work) or stool (at home), as we gaze at the ceiling or down our noses! It does not necessarily display arrogance when we are on our own, as we could just be thinking, but it does if we are with the follower and are supposed to be listening.

It's a posture that many of us adopt, but are resistant to recognizing as having arrogant overtones. It is interesting to note how we automatically remove our feet from the desk and change our stance, when our own boss comes in! In some oriental cultures, where the cult of the individual is less strong, it is a personal affront if you display the soles of your feet to a business colleague or acquaintance.

It is a self-centred style of 'listening', based on an assumption of superiority, and is very passive, as there is complete disinterest at both the logical and emotional levels. The body language is static as the posture will be maintained, whether we talk or listen. There is no positive eye contact, although we do not mind 'looking down our noses', the only way we can look in that position.

If our attention is eventually caught, then we will alter our postures and gestures, depending on whether or not we move into a logical listening, aggressive listening or listening interruptus mode.

If we take that deep breath and recognize what are we are doing and why, we can move into active listening.

Nervous listening

We manifest this when we are in an awkward situation – a job interview, appraisal interview, talking to a 'difficult boss' or client. Occasionally, we might manifest this with a follower, if we are being put under pressure.

We want to listen, we try to listen, but are only capable of listening to our heartbeat. This form of non-listening manifests itself in nervous gestures, which are also displayed when we have to talk. There is an almost infinite number of nervous gestures, and each person has a favourite. We usually do not know we are making them. It is a matter of great surprise to managers when they see themselves on video for the first time to recognize this reality. We fiddle with our fingers, we fiddle with our hair, we fiddle with our faces, we cover our mouths and move our forefinger up and down our top lips, we tap-dance under the table, we move our chairs and tickle our ears. The list goes on and on.

As an aside, developing the ability to notice another's involuntary gestures and, hence, their nervousness is a useful skill. If we want to generate empathy, we know we have a lot of work to do. If there has been verbal agreement to something we have said, we know that it was an involuntary agreement, unlikely to translate into action.

Our nervous listening will also be conveyed by the fact that we ask for information to be repeated, because we have not heard it properly, or by coming in with the answer to the wrong question.

As nervous listeners, there is little we can do, except take that deep breath, or breaths, to calm ourselves.

When the follower is behaving in this annoying manner, remember that it may well be nerves and try to calm them down.

A final point. Often, we try to control our nerves and our gestures and partially succeed. Assuming we are sitting down, the gestures move to our feet (the tap-dance or shuffle), which cannot be seen. What a keen observer will notice, however, is that we adopt a very rigid posture above the table.

HOW CAN WE BECOME BETTER LISTENERS?

There are seven key ways in which we can become better listeners.

Be committed

We need to recognize and believe in the power of effective listening – that, unless we listen effectively, we have wasted all those good questions. We have to want to listen 'actively'. 'Actively' is an excellent word, because it conveys the reality that we have to make a conscious move to listen well. As we now know, effective listening is not a passive thing, a meaning the word conveys, but a difficult skill, in which we need to engage our hearts and minds actively, if we are going to be effective and reap the rewards of our questions.

Be objective

We need to think, make that deliberate pause, and take that deep breath. As we have seen, it is our feelings, our opinions, our prejudices (whether against the follower or the content) or our nerves that deny us effective listening.

Just as good leaders learn how to take control, not of others, but of themselves, so too does the effective listener. Taking the time out as a discussion starts to say to ourselves, 'I am going to listen' will improve our skill. Deliberately pausing, when the comment comes that will trigger an instant negative logical or emotional response will improve our skill. In short, being proactive, not reactive.

Only when we have listened to ourselves can we listen effectively to the follower.

Suspend judgement

If we judge, we don't really listen. If we judge in the act of listening, there are two outcomes.

We disagree

If we don't want to express our disagreement, we will be turned off and lapse into passive listening, thus denying an effective conversation. This passive listening, if we are in the follower role, can lead to the outcome (which annoys so many bosses because they don't understand the reasons), where we verbally commit to doing things we don't believe in or want to do and so either do badly or not at all, if we can find a good excuse, later!

If we do express our disagreement, we will move into aggressive listening or listening interruptus and the subsequent flow from us of closed questions will deny an effective conversation.

We agree

That may seem fine, but early agreement will mean we lose the possibility of picking up on some little nuances or new angles because we have stopped listening.

Check for understanding

How often do both parties assume understanding, only to be rudely awakened subsequently by actions that are inconsistent with what was assumed? So, pause to recap and ensure you used the open question approach covered in the previous chapter.

Use positive body language

The words we speak account for around only 10 per cent of the total impact of a face-to-face communication. The way we speak – the tones, modulation, intensity, phrasing and use of pauses – makes for around 35 per cent of the total impact, and our body language – our gestures, posture and facial expression – a highly significant 55 per cent.

If we are listening effectively, then we will display the right body language. If we consciously try to use the right body language, we will probably feel awkward, but we will be better listeners. 'Conscious incompetence' will lead, with practise, to 'conscious competence' and, eventually, 'unconscious competence' or natural ability. 'Rubbish!', I hear some of you say. Not at all. It is why people being trained in good telephone technique are told to smile. When they do, the tone of their voice becomes warmer, and this is picked up at the other end of the phone.

So, let us now consider:

❑ facial expression;
❑ gestures;
❑ body posture.

Facial expression

Our facial expressions should reflect the feelings of the person talking to us. If the follower is feeling sad, look sad, if happy, look happy, and if angry, look angry – angry together at the source of the speaker's anger.

If you are the source of anger, however, that's a different kettle of fish. The speaker will get the impression that you are angry with them if you adopt an angry expression, which is likely to be the case. This is the moment for the assertive pause, not the angry response.

If there are no emotions being expressed, as the speaker is in logical mode, then look confident and thoughtful – you are both in thinking mode together.

There should be fairly frequent eye contact, but never a glare nor stare. Such eye contact stops you becoming distracted and conveys the message that you are, in fact, all ears.

Gestures

Gestures are for the speaker, not the listener. By using appropriate gestures, the impact of the message of the speaker is significantly enhanced. Gestures on the part of the listener, however, are simply distracting – a form of non-verbal interruption.

Posture

Now, there is not a single right posture, as this will vary according to the situation – the logic or emotion being expressed, the ebb and flow of the conversation. However, in all situations, an assertive posture should be adopted, rather than an aggressive or a submissive one. For instance, when seated, the listener could take up an open position (neither legs nor arms folded), leaning forward slightly, with the head a little to one side, and hands clasped loosely together, resting on the lap. There are variations on this, such as leaning back slightly (to accommodate the other person leaning forward), with an open posture, one hand on the chin and the other supporting the elbow, or sitting straight with legs slightly apart, each hand resting on the appropriate knee. This last position is the best position for the back, and is known as the Pharaoh's posture.

Another way of deciding on an effective posture is to con-sciously avoid all the postures covered under poor listening!

Use words

An effective listener uses words that have the right tone to convey the right meaning. There are two aspects to this:

❑ reflection;
❑ interest.

Reflection

As we have seen, we should use our faces to reflect the speaker's feelings. Equally, the words and tone can support this if we paraphrase the words or reflect the feelings of the speaker.

Interest

Show interest, too, by making those little verbal noises or even words that convey this. The murmur 'mmmmhuh' (or variations, which I will not try to spell) or 'Well, I never', 'You don't say' or simply 'I agree'.

Appreciate silence

We tend to dislike silence and rush in to fill it with words. However, in fact, silence can be a very powerful way to uncover truth. At a judicious moment, when we have asked a searching question and received a short, unsatisfactory response or we have made a telling statement, we fall silent until the follower speaks. What will often happen at such times is that the follower will reveal what they have tried to conceal. They rush in to fill that awkward pause. They are very consciously concerned about the silence. They are emotionally distracted and so what they were trying consciously to conceal slips out or, at the very least, a veil is removed that, if we are listening effectively, we can pick up on and probe.

However, this reality has more to do with effective interviewing skills than it does with effective listening skills. The main point is that a natural discomfort with silence may often impair our active listening, either because we do not pause to collect our thoughts and give a measured response or ask the right question or we speak when it would have better, from the other person's point of view, if we had remained silent.

We can, by being silent, give them time to control their emotions or gather their thoughts, or simply share together a pleasant mood or ambience.

As Mozart said, 'Silence is the most profound sound in music'.
Remember that just as bad listening destroys the power of the
right question, without the right question you have little opportunity to listen actively. The two skills are inextricably interlinked.
If you want to improve the quality, and effectiveness, of all your
key relationships (not only the relationship with the follower),
you have to develop both in tandem. Doing this is a powerful
way of improving your own creative thinking skills as well as
those of your followers, and creativity is the subject of the next
chapter.

7

DEVELOPING CREATIVITY

In this final chapter on skills, we look at how using specific question combinations can improve our creativity and innovation and how, as leaders, we can improve the innovation of both an individual follower or team. We look first at the 'Why not?'/ 'How?' combination and from that derive the group discovery technique (GDT), then at 'Why?'/'Why?', 'How?'/'How?', 'What?'/'How?' and 'What?'/'Why?'.

'WHY NOT?'/'HOW?'

We have already seen this combination in action with the Alaskan Electricity example (see page 49), when it was used to find a single action area from the root cause of the problem. The symptom was the negative effect on profits, caused by the cost of work teams addressing the root problem, which was ice and snow breaking overhead cables. Recalling the sequence, we had:

'Why not shake the poles?'
'How can we shake the poles?'
'Why not use bears to shake the poles?'
'How do we motivate the bears to shake the poles?'
'Why not put meat on top of the poles?'
'How do get meat to the top of the poles?'
'Why not use helicopters to put the meat on top of the poles?'
'Why not forget the bears and use the helicopters to sweep away the ice and snow before it breaks the cables?'

Similarly, if poor quality was the one cause of loss of sale revenue, a 'Why not?'/'How?' sequence could be:

'Why not improve the quality of the product?'
'How can we do that?'
'Why not ensure staff are more committed to eradicating quality defects?'
'How can we do that?'
'Why don't we give them more responsibility and autonomy?'
'How can we do that?'
'Why don't we develop self-managing teams, which are allowed to implement any quality improvements they determine are relevant?'

Further analysis leads to recognition of the need for and power of the group discovery technique (GDT).

GROUP DISCOVERY TECHNIQUE (GDT)

Looking back to the Alaskan Electricity example, what do you think would have happened to the development of the idea if the response by one group member to the first suggestion had been, 'With respect, there are over a 1000 miles of poles, so that suggestion simply won't work'?

Again, assuming the first criticism did not emerge until the suggestion that bears should shake the poles had been made, and it was along the lines of 'With respect, that simply won't work. I have carried out extensive research, and there are only three polar bears in Alaska', what might have happened?

Criticism destroys creativity, and often leads to the one right answer – that of the leader! Usually that result is not intended at the outset. It is simply that the more logical we are (and we are all brought up to communicate verbally in logical sequences), the more we have developed our critical faculties. We can instantly see flaws in any idea. So, we have to apply and enforce a simple rule on ourselves and our followers if we want to have/develop a range of ideas:

During the exploration phase (which need only last 10 to 15 minutes), no criticism is allowed, in word or body language form.

Criticism must be left to the evaluation stage.

Furthermore, it is not sufficient to simply avoid the negative as otherwise you just get a number of undeveloped suggestions from different individuals. Everyone should deliberately suspend judgement (which is a key to effective listening as we know) and help each other to develop the initial suggestion into a sound action.

It is the combination of questioning and listening that leads to discovery. By using the GDT whenever you or the group asks an open question, you guarantee that the group's combined power exceeds the sum of the individual contributions and achieve that rare reality in the workplace, synergy.

'WHY'?/'WHY?'

Let us now look at Figure 7.1. There are two key points to make about it.

First, as pointed out in Chapter 5, the actual phrasing of the question is important. We would not use a bald 'why?', but the more open question 'What could all the possible reasons be for...' followed by the issue or problem under consideration. We need to encourage what is termed 'thinking outside the box' – that is breaking free of the usual assumptions and mind-sets we all fall into so as to develop new insights and angles. This is permitted, nay desirable, when we are exploring and before we evaluate.

So, we phrase the question in such a way to enable us and others to come forward with all sorts of possibilities. This increases the probability that, as we develop each initial sub-issue with another 'What could all the possible reasons be for...', we will come up with a set of reasons or causes that are more all-embracing than would otherwise be the case.

Second, a cause is also a possible solution – either an action area or an alternative action. So, by following the 'Why?'/'Why?'

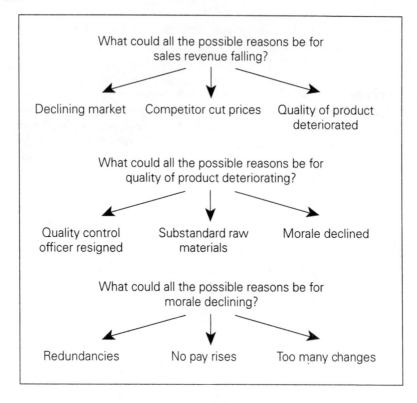

What could all the possible reasons be for sales revenue falling?

Declining market   Competitor cut prices   Quality of product deteriorated

What could all the possible reasons be for quality of product deteriorating?

Quality control officer resigned   Substandard raw materials   Morale declined

What could all the possible reasons be for morale declining?

Redundancies   No pay rises   Too many changes

Figure 7.1 *'Why?'/'Why?'*

approach, we are uncovering a set of solutions at the same time! Thus, taking our first example in Figure 7.1, and accepting that there could be a much wider range of causes at each level, let us assume that the market is expanding and there has been no competitor price war, so we know that we need to improve the quality of the product to reverse the decline in sales. We already have a set of options to consider as to how to do that, because we have followed the causal chain down.

'HOW?'/'HOW?'

This is the traditional creative thinking route, and an example can be found in Figure 7.2. Again, I have two points I would like to make.

First, rather than using the bland 'how?', I suggest asking a question that focuses on action (the end product of creativity) as well as encouraging exploration, which is 'What are all the possible actions we could take to...' followed by the area to be improved. In Figure 7.2, the first example of such an area is that of increasing the sales revenue.

Second, when we use the question 'What are all the possible actions we could take to...', we may well come up with more action areas than specific actions. So, we apply the long version of the 'How?', until it is obvious that it is no longer the right question. At that point, in fact, a different open question needs to be asked to achieve the detail required for implementation.

So, at the first level of use of the question for our first example in Figure 7.2, we have the answer 'Cut prices'. This is the end action area as using the question again, 'What are all the actions we could take to cut prices?', is a nonsense question. However, for the purposes of implementation or decision making, we would need to ask different questions, such as 'By what amount?' and 'What variations of prices would be necessary over our product range?' In real life, research would be needed to determine what level of price cut for each product would maximize the increase in revenue.

Equally, at the first level for our second example in Figure 7.2, we have 'What are all the possible actions we could take to improve motivation of sales staff?' As this is still an action area, we can apply this long form of the 'How?' question and get a series of answers. We continue this process until we have an action area where a different type of question needs to be used. As shown, 'training' is an action response to the question 'What are all the possible actions we can take to improve team working?' and the final questions to enable action planning or implementation of training are 'What sort?', 'When?' and 'By whom?'

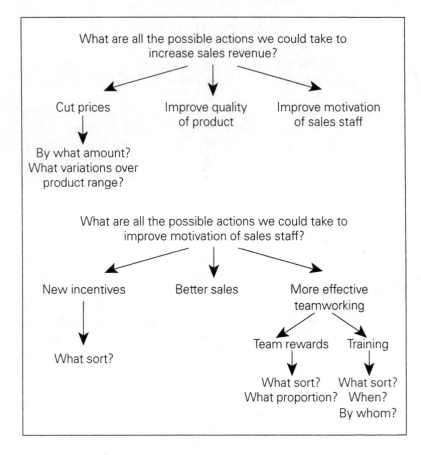

Figure 7.2 *'How?'/'How?'*

'WHAT?'/'HOW?'

Figure 7.3 shows the technique known as force field analysis. Like most creative-thinking or problem-solving techniques it boils down to asking open questions.

Any change to be introduced or situation to be improved is the issue. As an example, we could take use of a networked system. The current use would be a position of dynamic equilibrium, held

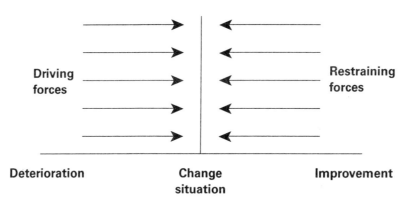

- What are all the possible driving/restraining forces?
- What are the priorities?
- What are all the possible actions we can take ('How?') to reduce the impact of the key restraining forces/increase the impact of the key driving forces?

Figure 7.3 *'What?'/'How?' – force field analysis*

in balance by the impact of two opposing forces – restraining forces and driving forces. The restraining forces push towards deterioration – in this case, less use of the system – and the driving forces push for improvement – greater use.

If the power of a single restraining force is reduced or the power of single driving force increased, the balance point (in this case the degree of use) will shift in the improvement direction. Therefore, having identified the end goal to be achieved over a certain time period, continuous improvement can be made to achieve it. The initial process, which can be repeated regularly, involves asking a series of open questions and looking at the answers.

Identify forces

First, ask the question 'What are all the possible driving forces?' Examples would include enthusiastic support staff, a champion, a business need, customer demand, easy access and so on.

Then ask 'What are all the possible restraining forces?' These could be fear of technology, lack of databases, poor training, poor understanding of benefits, poor system coordination and so on.

Prioritize

The next step is to ask 'What are the most important driving/ restraining forces?' It is wise to limit yourself or the team to no more than two key driving forces/restraining forces. Otherwise you will end up with too many things to do. In a team situation, the easiest way to prioritize is for each individual to select their top two, and use a scoring system to determine the two overall favourites.

Note – all these techniques can be done individually or with a small team.

Action plan

Now apply the 'How?'/'How?' approach (but using the action phrasing) to develop action plans to reduce or eliminate the impact of the two key restraining forces, and to increase the effectiveness of the two key driving forces (or introduce one or two new driving forces that were discovered in the initial exploration phase).

'WHAT?'/'WHY?'

This is a simple and powerful technique that recognizes we all make assumptions, some of which can be invalid.

So, when considering a problem or issue, we need to follow this simple process.

❑ **Identify.** What are all the assumptions we could be making?
❑ **Check validity.** Why are we making them?
❑ **Remove invalid assumptions.**
❑ **Discover better solutions.**

Now we have discovered techniques that will enable us to be more effective questioners and listeners, and how to apply questioning combinations, using the GDT, to be more creative ourselves and to guarantee synergy in any group we lead, we turn to another key responsibility of an effective leader – improving staff performance.

8

IMPROVING STAFF PERFORMANCE

If we refer back to Chapter 1, one of the effective leader's key roles is 'putting work into context'.

In this chapter, we consider how you, as an effective leader, can ensure that your followers focus on the key areas of their jobs, prioritize their work flows and how performance standards can be put in place – the basis for monitoring, review and delivering continuous improvement.

FOCUSING ON KEY AREAS

Take a look at Figure 8.1.

The elephant stands for a core business goal of the job being considered, and an ant stands for a trivial work activity – a meeting, a phone call, an information flow, interruption and so on that does not add value.

Many followers and leaders alike can find themselves not addressing their elephants and spending far too much time killing ants, which produces little meat for the table.

By catching the elephants, prioritizing work flows and eliminating ants, the follower will carry out their job both efficiently and effectively. We look at each in turn in this section, before considering how to improve performance.

Figure 8.1 *Elephants and ants*

Catching the elephants

This involves a four-step process:

- ❑ define the elephants;
- ❑ set objectives;
- ❑ set interim milestones;
- ❑ determine activities.

Let us look at each in the order given.

Define the elephants

Look at each job and determine the core goals.

Note that this process should be shared with the follower. Indeed, if you have a team, it would be best for this to be a team exercise as going through it together will ensure that potential overlaps are eliminated. Two causes of demotivation and inefficiency are where there is no clarity of role or overlaps occur that lead to conflict.

As an example, we will assume you are a training manager and have a number of training officers. One is responsible for skills training, and together you are clarifying this follower's role.

Elephants in this scenario might be to:

❏ deliver skills training;
❏ ensure individual development needs are met;
❏ ensure organizational needs are met;
❏ provide added value.

Set objectives

Elephants never die – the core goals remain with the job, unless there is a change in role or requirements. To be able to focus effectively, each goal must have an objective (or objectives). Objectives must be SMART, that is:

❏ specific;
❏ measurable;
❏ agreed;
❏ realistic;
❏ timed.

The usual time period for work objectives is a year. By way of example, if we look at 'deliver skills training', the annual target could be a certain number of days – say 100 – that have to completed. With 'provide added value', an assessment form could be devised for the delegates to provide feedback, with a 1 to 10 scale for the various categories and a target set of achieving an average of 7.5 by year end.

Set interim milestones

Monthly or quarterly targets can be derived from each objective. In fact, once a measurement system is in place, there can be continuous monitoring of progress.

Determine activities

The activities that relate to the elephants can be derived easily. For instance, for the first objective, 'provide skills training', process and programme design, and actual delivery are core activities.

Prioritizing work flows

The chart shown in Figure 8.2 will help each follower prioritize effectively.

The chart is self-explanatory, though we will look at ant elimination strategies below. Without such planning and prioritization, what happens normally is that the elephants, which are important but not urgent, are either never addressed or only addressed when they have moved to the left – that is, they have become urgent and important! So, for instance, staff development (if the follower is also a leader), coaching and delegation – in fact, many of the activities of a proactive and effective leader – are permanently left on the back burner.

	Urgent	Non-urgent
Important	Part of an elephant Do now	Part of an elephant Do a little each day
Not important	An ant Do quickly now	An ant Ignore, delegate or reduce

Figure 8.2 *Prioritizing work flows*

By slicing up the non-urgent elephants – that is, by developing a plan whereby your follower does a little each day or each week, using the time released by effective prioritization and ant elimination – the quality of work done will improve significantly, and, overall, the time taken to do the work will reduce.

Eliminating the ants

There are various strategies that are relevant to both you and your followers for eliminating ants. It is crucial to implement these as, otherwise, there can be no effective focus on the elephants.

We shall look at ignoring them, delegating them and reducing their impact.

Ignoring them

There can be a danger that we do everything we are asked to do because we want to be seen to be effective – please clients, please the boss, help a colleague and so on. This is fatal to focus. A very sound policy – given that so many people think they are dealing with an elephant that is, in fact, an ant – is to wait for the first reminder. Clearly, you have to use your judgement and never adopt this for elephants.

I still recall my boss, with whom I was lunching, waxing lyrical about what he had heard IBM was doing on the training front. At the end of the meal, he asked me to carry out detailed research and produce a paper on the implications. I dutifully said 'Yes' and waited for the first reminder.

He asked me five years ago, and retired a year ago!

Now, of course, you are the leader, so a critical implication is that you do not delegate ants in the guise of elephants.

Delegating them

There is a view that nothing should be done at one level in an organization if it can be done equally well at a lower level. I don't completely subscribe to this as it means that all the rubbish is dumped down, which is against effective teamworking and demotivates the follower.

However, provided you are coaching the follower so that they can take on part of one of your elephants – that is, growing their job and saving you time – then you can delegate away some of your ants as well.

Reducing their impact

There are ways to reduce the impact of the ants in our working lives. Specifically:

- ❑ managing expectations;
- ❑ using systems;
- ❑ grouping them.

Managing expectations. Most leaders, in order to be available, have an open door policy for their followers. It is a good idea to set aside a few hours each week to focus on elephants, but advise your followers in advance.

Additionally, many followers bring you problems to solve, but often, for you, they are very antish ones. For the sake of follower development, and saving you time, I would recommend that you tell your followers that, if they have any problems, they should bring them to you, but only after they have thought out the solution(s) to those problems. By doing this, you will often be rubber-stamping their answers (which takes little time) or, at the very least, have a base of ideas to develop to provide the solution.

Finally, if you have part shares in or all of a secretary, he/she can be developed to deal with many, many of your ants.

Using systems. Technology is a great blessing in this regard – there are electronic diaries, electronic action lists and so on. You can identify the ants and parts of elephants for the week/day according to the prioritization methodology and use electronic planners – to put on the goals, objectives, milestones and so on.

Grouping them. This is a straightforward technique. Dealing with all the post in one go (prioritizing), putting the making of calls on hold for a couple of hours, then dealing with them in one go, arranging a day of sales visits or meetings and so on.

The result?

By adopting these approaches, you should be able to find chunks of quality time to focus on elephants. In our normal working lives, we can suffer endless interruptions and distractions, with the result that the quality of work is much poorer and the time taken (recovering from each interruption) much longer than if we can focus uninterrupted.

IMPROVING STAFF PERFORMANCE

We cannot manage what we cannot measure. By ensuring that key goals are derived for each job, together with smart objectives and interim milestones, the leader has the means to measure performance.

What is required is a reporting system that occurs on a monthly basis and shows how the follower is actually performing. The leader can then review the data and acts according to the three possible outcomes:

❑ performance is below standard in one area or more;
❑ performance is standard;
❑ performance is above standard in one area or more.

We shall deal with each in turn.

Performance below standard

You have to meet the follower to find out the reasons for this and agree what actions you need to take or need to do to support his or her improvement. It is infinitely better for corrective action to be agreed after one month, than the problem be discovered at the annual appraisal!

Performance is standard

Acknowledgement only is required with 'keep up the good work' and so on.

Performance above standard

A personal visit with heart-warming words of praise being spoken.

Note that it is a good management practice to hold quarterly review meetings. These help you to stay in touch and help performance, at whatever level, to move a notch higher.

In these first eight chapters, we have concentrated in the main on the one-to-one relationship between leader and follower. If you can build a high-performance team, then you will have to spend considerably less time on individual relationships as well as improving the performance of each individual team member, including yourself.

We look at building a team in the next chapter.

9

BUILDING A TEAM

In this chapter, we look at the question 'Why build a team?', what an effective team looks like, and what key actions a team-builder should undertake to build a high-performance team. For a more in-depth study, I would refer you to another of my books in this series, *How to be a Better Team-builder* (see the Bibliography).

WHY BUILD A TEAM?

The reasons are simple. An effective team is the most powerful way to develop the individual and to maximize business performance.

As Anthony Montebello and Victor Buzzotta said, 'Companies that are willing to rethink old ways and develop teams can profit by increasing quality and productivity. And they can develop a workforce that is motivated and committed'.

Tom Peters said, 'I observe that the power of the team is so great that it is often wise to violate common sense and force a team structure on almost anything... companies that do will achieve a greater focus, stronger task orientation, more innovation and enhanced individual commitment'.

Finally, research by the American Society of Training and Development found that companies that developed a team approach saw productivity, quality, customer and job satisfaction improve, and an increased ability of team members to resolve disputes themselves.

WHAT DOES AN EFFECTIVE TEAM LOOK LIKE?

If you are going to build an effective team, you need to know what one looks like.

To acquire this knowledge, grab paper and pencil or pen, think back to all the meetings you have been to in your working life and list all the factors that demotivated you, that made you wish you were somewhere else.

Once you have done that, then reverse all these negatives to produce the positives. You will find that you have painted a picture of an effective team – and a wonderful picture it is.

Figure 9.1 shows the aspects that make a team ineffective. The words shown summarize the views of groups of managers who have taken part in the exercise above.

Figure 9.2 gives a snapshot of an effective team. See how the negatives have been reversed to produce a high performance team. The key question is, how can we turn this vision into reality?

WHAT A TEAM-BUILDER NEEDS TO DO

Here are my top ten tips for becoming an effective team-builder.

Believe in yourself

Only when we are confident in our own abilities, have developed our self-esteem and become at ease with ourselves will we have the capability to focus externally and build others. These are exactly the same attitudes as are required to be an effective leader.

Believe in your team members

We have to have faith in the potential of all our team members – suspend judgement, as it were, and provide each member with the environment and opportunity to fulfil the potential that is always there. However, sometimes, because of upbringing and experience, some people can be locked into low levels of

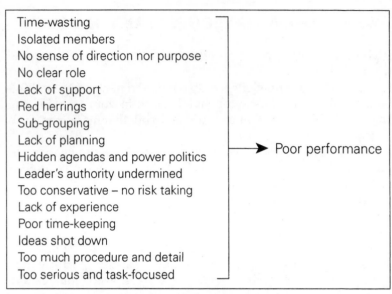

Figure 9.1 *The ineffective team*

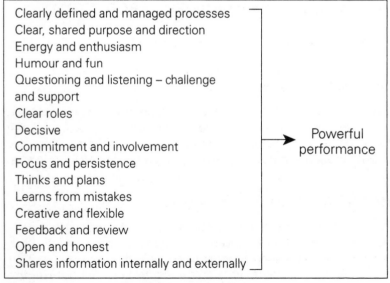

Figure 9.2 *The effective team*

self-esteem, do not believe in themselves and perceive themselves to be and are, incompetent.

Provided you have exercised your duty of care – provided the path to competence – then if there is no real response over time, you have to take action to remove the individual from the team. Otherwise, that one individual will deny the rest of the team the opportunity to develop into a high-performing team.

Use the group discovery technique (GDT)

This technique (see page 72) promotes discovery, provided the rule of no criticism in either word or body language form is rigorously applied in the exploration phase. In fact, introducing this technique is the single best way to build an effective team because it gene-rates the behaviours that are the hallmark of high-performance teams. These are good questioning and listening skills within an atmosphere of challenge with support. In fact, I know of an effect-ive team that was built solely using this technique.

Over a decade ago now, I learnt this technique on a develop-ment programme and decided to introduce it in my own team. I had to sell it to the boss, who was not a believer in teams and not a people person. So, I applied the PBA rule. PBA stands for perceived balance of advantage. What this means is that any person will be persuaded to do something, provided they perceive a net balance of advantage in it for them. One implication of this is that you sell an idea or whatever from the other party's perspective and value system, not your own (for more details, see my book *The Power of Persuasion: Improving your performance and leadership skills*). As a result, I did the boss a paper, explaining the technique and focusing on how it would increase quality and quantity of output. He agreed and I facilitated the first run.

The first idea came from the most junior member of the team, and it was instantly criticized non-verbally by the boss! Very delicately I said, 'I know, George, that you did not mean to, but you have criticized Pauline non-verbally, and we have all agreed not to do that'. He stopped, and the session went on to be a great success. Thereafter, using GDT became a way of life. In fact, any one of us could call whoever was around to help out with a

problem that arose in the course of working through our individual tasks. What is more, the boss recognized that teamworking
was a very good thing and was personally delighted at how
creative he could be. He was very logical and thought he was not
creative. Indeed, he started to chair meetings on a rota basis and
setting objectives became a team exercise and was no longer
mandated by him one on one. We also starting socializing together
and so on.

And all this happened thanks to GDT!

Identify and play to strengths

This is vital to build confidence early on. Professor Drucker once
said that there is a defect in many Western cultures when it comes
to selecting people for jobs – this being a tendency to focus on
any weaknesses and select the person with the fewest of them,
rather than identify the key strengths required to do the job and
select the person who matches these requirements most closely,
ignoring any weaknesses they may have that will not affect job
performance.

Later, when cohesion and confidence have grown, further new
skills should be developed.

Meet regularly

If it is practical, meet once a week – Friday afternoon or Monday
morning – to review, share experiences, refocus energies and
provide mutual support.

Use process

The power of process cannot be overstated. Process should be
deployed to build the team and define and complete the task.
The GDT technique can be used to discover and agree the right
processes to be applied. GDT is, of course, a process in itself and
involves two steps:

❑   agree the question;
❑   explore it without criticism for an agreed time.

As examples, set out below are two processes: the first to build a team vision and values, and the second to complete a team task.

Building a team vision and values

Figure 9.3 illustrates a process a team can work through to establish its own vision and the set of values it will uphold in its day-to-day work.

An example of a vision and value statement is as follows:

Our team, when effective, will:

Have a clear, shared sense of direction and purpose with enthusiastic, committed team members who are all involved and participate. We will focus on achieving stretching and demanding tasks and goals, supporting and helping each other develop and grow our individual strengths. We will have fun together, and be able to question and challenge each other so that the team and the individual can continuously improve.

The core values that will help us become an effective team are openness, honesty, mutual respect, trust, sharing and humour.

Completing a team task

In Figure 9.4, a process is set out that can be used to complete a team task.

Initially you would be the process coordinator, but as the team matures, you might want to rotate the role.

Depending on your leadership style, you might want to explain the process, receive feedback and modify so that it is the team's process or 'promote discovery'. This involves asking 'What are the things we should do in what order to complete this project?', steering the dicussion if needs be. Critical aspects are that the process needs to be planned before simply diving into the task and every team member needs to agree to it.

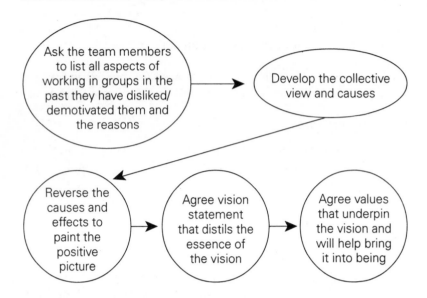

Figure 9.3 *A process to create a team vision and values*

Promote feedback

As we know, this will motivate and improve performance, but only when the team has developed cohesion. Otherwise, it will be taken as criticism and destroy the team. Let the individual lead the discussion of what they do well, what could be improved and how.

Develop vision and values

It is vital that the team knows what success looks like, so develop the vision and values for the team before focusing on the task. Often, team builders have a natural and understandable drive to get the task done. Just as many companies are developing a vision and values for all employees, as they help provide focus and motivate, so you, the leader, should ensure that these are developed for the team.

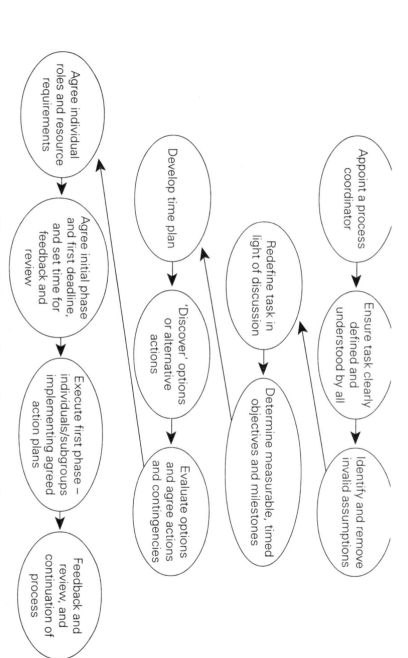

Figure 9.4 *A process for completing a team task*

Remember your role

Your role is as a coordinator of a process rather than a controller of people You create the environment in which discovery can occur and success be achieved.

Finally, promote humour and enjoy yourself. An effective team is the most exhilarating experience we are ever likely to have in the workplace.

Having looked at teams, in the next chapter we consider how to manage change effectively.

10

REACTING TO CHANGE

In this, the first of two chapters on change, we focus on how we react to change and what strategies we, as followers and leaders, can follow to ensure that a reactive approach can be transformed to a proactive approach.

HOW DO YOU REACT TO CHANGE?

Let us start by promoting discovery in you, rather than simply telling you the answer.

I would like you to think back to an occasion when you experienced a change that was sudden, either in its announcement or in the occurrence, and which you perceived negatively. Examples include receiving unexpected criticism about an area you thought yourself competent in from someone you trusted and whose opinion you respected or being advised that you were being made redundant or being told by a former partner that they were finishing the relationship – any change that was sudden, affected you personally and was perceived negatively. Unfortunately, there is bound to be some such change in your past.

Once you have recalled the change, take a pen or pencil and piece of paper and write down your feelings, thoughts and actions – but separate them into three timeframes.

☐ *immediate* the instant of the occurrence or announcement;
☐ *short-term* hours and days after;
☐ *long-term* looking back after months or years.

If you could complete this exercise before carrying on reading, that would be very helpful as otherwise there will be no discovery.

When I ask groups of managers to carry out this exercise, they invariably describe what is termed the transition or reaction curve (see Figure 10.1). I would imagine that you will have done likewise.

The curve charts how we react to sudden, negative change, the phases of that reaction we go through over time, and the impact those phases have on our self-esteem. The assumption is that we start off fairly high on the self-esteem level – we have quite a strong belief in our self-worth, our competence and our capability. If you like, we are quite mature. Then the change occurs and the curve is created by the following phases of our reactions to that change.

Shock and denial

The first reaction to a sudden, negative change is one of shock. The suddenness, coupled with the lack of continuity, means that there is no connection between it and our existing mental model of reality. We have had no prior warning nor expectation of the event. Our reaction is purely instinctive and 'animal'. We are caught like a rabbit in the sudden glare of the headlights of a car and freeze.

We do not necessarily believe the incredible – we deny the actuality that, at that moment in time, has no meaning. This is usually a short-lived phase, but not necessarily so. The key factors at play are:

❑ the nature of the sudden change;
❑ the degree of evidence supporting the new change;
❑ our maturity.

You may have noticed how the curve in Figure 10.1 moves upwards slightly in this phase. Many years ago now, a large company decided to shut down one of its many production units, and the then General Manager was told to summon the workers and tell them that they were losing their jobs in six months' time when the factory would be closed.

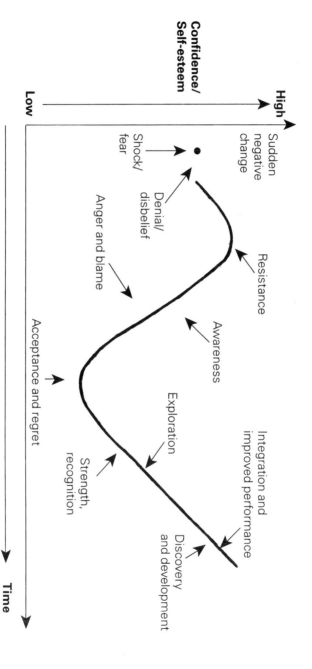

Figure 10.1 *The transition or reaction curve*

For the first six weeks after the announcement they achieved record production levels, denying this horrible future and trying to prove that their unit should be saved.

Resistance and awareness

Assuming that we move beyond denial, then we will resist the dawning of the new, unpleasant reality. We are starting a process of integrating the new with the old and initially we have to resist the change so that the we can close the gap slowly. It is important, when we are responsible for the shock, that we understand this and have all the evidence at our disposal to overcome this inevitable resistance.

Sometimes we can be too logical and emotional ourselves – 'Don't you believe me? I wouldn't lie to you. Are you calling me a liar?' and so on.

Resistance is also inevitable because we are subconsciously fighting the descent to a lower level of self-esteem. When we are sacked, we lose self-esteem, we lose confidence and our competence declines. We become more insecure. Few seek out that reality. For example, a professional was made redundant during the recession. She was very competent, but the organization had decided that, because of cost-cutting necessitated by the recession, her function was no longer required. She was clearly advised that this was the reason for her being let go, but for some time felt that it was because she was incompetent.

Evidence to the contrary played a strong part in overcoming that perception: the organization subsequently used her services as an independent, and paid her roughly twice the amount she had received when she had been a salaried member of staff!

Anger and blame

As our awareness that this change represents a new reality grows, as our resistance is overcome, we remain gripped by emotion. The emotion associated with shock is fear – an inevitable consequence of the high level of uncertainty that the event instantly generates. At this point, the emotion is one of anger and blame.

We 'rail against fate', and that anger can be both internally and externally focused.

A part of self-blame that can linger into and beyond acceptance is regret – 'If only, I had…'. How often do children blame themselves, their perceived incompetence and inadequacy, for their parents' divorce? How often does regret for the passing of good times stay with us for ever?

A confident extrovert tends to blame others, and get the balance wrong. A less confident introvert tends to blame themselves, and, equally, gets the balance wrong.

Blame is a necessary, but fundamentally counter-productive, phase associated with the emotional response in this kind of situation.

If we were operating at a high level of self-esteem before the sudden change, then the blame phase tends to be temporary and not too intense. This a fundamental point in terms of the shape of the curve. The higher our pre-existing self-esteem, the quicker the transition and the shallower the dip in terms of loss of confidence and self-esteem. There is, unfortunately, an element of the virtuous and the vicious in our reactions to sudden negative change. The lower our self-esteem, the more vicious our reaction to it and the higher our self-esteem the more virtuous we are likely to be about it.

Acceptance

For most of us, we will move on to acceptance, eventually – it can be hours, days, weeks, months or years. However, the nature of that acceptance and the extent to which it is a temporary phase on a downward or upward path will vary.

Recognition of the likely reaction curve is critically important as it enables us to move from unconscious incompetence (at the mercy of the winds of reaction we do not recognize) to conscious incompetence (knowing why what is happening is happening, which gives the possibility of our cerebral side intervening positively).

Exploration, discovery and integration

Provided the nature of our acceptance has a rational and positive dimension, then we will move into the exploration phase. We have to fight to be rational, to accentuate the positive we do not feel, to seek support, retain balance, force out blame and replace it with detached understanding, and thereby preserve as much self-esteem as we can. We must let the heart weep (mourning is vital), but force the head to change the heart.

So, the key to the ascent upwards in the growth phase is to explore and evaluate from the base of acceptance, but not on our own, with others. Then, we can discover new meaning and develop new skills. We can use those hidden strengths that adversity brings closer to the surface, but which we need to consciously uncover and tap into.

Finally, we need to integrate the new learning with the past, which was so suddenly changed. We need to review and reflect – to look back, not in anger, but with understanding.

Having looked at the curve in some detail, we now turn to how, as leaders, we can produce maximum gain with minimum pain.

MAXIMIZING GAIN

Here we look at how to ensure we are at the right phase before 'selling on', then how to persuade our followers to accept change and, finally, consider how to maximize gain for the team.

Moving to the right phase

If there has been some organizational announcement, which you perceive as having negative aspects, then you will start descending down the reaction curve. The problem is that you have a duty as leader to sell on. Whenever I ask managers how effective they will be if they are sitting in the 'anger and blame' phase, they all reply 'useless'. So, you have to get yourself to the sunny uplands before you can sell the change to your subordinates. There are five actions that will help you do this.

❑ Use the assertive pause to control your emotions.
❑ If only the 'what' has been advised, seek out your boss, or whomsoever knows, to find out the 'why'. If we fully understand the thinking behind any change, it will often make sense.
❑ Seek support, especially if you are an introvert. You may have a work colleague you can trust or a partner or friend.
❑ Try to envision those sunny uplands – paint a picture of the change having been successfully introduced.
❑ Focus all the time on all the benefits that any change brings in its wake.

Helping the individual follower

If you can promote 'discovery' or change in the follower or team, that is by far the best strategy. Again, it is amazing how, often, if we ask the right questions and get people to work things out for themselves, they will reach the same conclusions as we have. So, if it is feasible and there is enough time, try to go the 'promote discovery' route.

Often this is not feasible, however. Everyone (including the leader) has been advised at the same time, there is no time and so on. In these kinds of cases, don't take it personally when an extrovert has a go at you. Simply give a full explanation of the thinking and share your vision of success, accentuating all the positive aspects, from the follower's perspective.

Whatever the circumstances, provide support, acknowledge their emotions, answer all questions asked and allow time. You may have to repeat the key messages on more than one occasion. If at all possible, allow them to be involved in the 'how'.

Maximizing gain for the team

When an event occurs suddenly that affects the team as a whole, each individual will descend down the reaction curve in their own way, and the team will be in danger of falling apart. Such an event could be an external shock – changed deadlines, IT system failing, sudden loss of a team member – or an internal one – a team member makes a mistake, say.

Let me give you a powerful example of this. A group of managers were trying to complete a two-day business simulation as one of a number of teams on a development programme.

This particular group had sailed through the early phases. They were carrying out the role of a subsidiary board running a pharmaceutical manufacturing company. The information had been digested and shared. The overall vision developed. A strategic plan had been devised, objectives had been set and performance indicators and policies were in place.

They had to make quarterly decisions, spanning three years, and had to input into the computer the first two decisions. Delighted with the results, which exceeded expectations, the five were grouped together around the computer, having just input the third quarter's decision. They displayed all the hallmarks of a performing team – energy, commitment, focus, humour and very positive body language.

The results flashed up on the screen. Five pairs of eyes followed the screen down to the profit or loss figure for the quarter – not necessarily the sole yardstick for success, but one that all groups treat as king. They were expecting a modest profit. They saw a thumping great loss, in excess of £250,000.

Within less than a minute, the team had totally fragmented. The Managing Director of the group told me in no uncertain terms what he thought of the simulation. He was an extrovert, quickly accepted the evidence of 'failure' and was allocating blame externally to the group. The Personnel Director disappeared to the toilet. The Finance Director went to a corner of the room, shaking his head in disbelief, clutching the printouts to his chest. The Production Director and Sales Director entered a 'healthy dialogue' where each blamed the other for the debacle.

Now, assuming you were this team's leader or Managing Director, what should you do? My suggestions would be the following.

❑ Try to control your emotions, using the assertive pause technique. Until you are in control of yourself, you have no hope of controlling the situation and building the team back to better performance.

❑ Call a review meeting.

❑ Acknowledge the emotions team members are feeling, point out the inevitable temporary fragmentation of the team – the descent into an overly individualistic and ego-centred state.

❑ Suggest actions individuals or subgroups can take to review the data and consider the reasons behind the loss (or whatever the problem is – generalizing). Emphasize the need to move away from blame and personalization, however understandable that is.

❑ Agree a meeting of the whole team in short order, where a team-based analysis of cause and effect can take place, using the base of research and thought individuals and subgroups have carried out.

❑ At the meeting, lead the discovery of the cause or causes and agree the actions required to remedy the situation.

Having considered how we react to sudden change and how to maximize gain, we turn in the next chapter to looking at your change preference and the implications.

11

UNDERSTANDING YOUR CHANGE PREFERENCES

In this chapter, there is a short questionnaire to complete that examines your change preferences. We also consider how we operate in each mode, the implications of different profiles, the differences between men and women, the impact on working relationships, and the need to focus on strengths and develop compensating strategies for weakness. We conclude by considering the team dimension.

PRODUCING YOUR PROFILE

To produce your profile, please complete the questionnaire set out on pages 107–9, following the guidelines.

Questionnaire on change preference

For each of the areas covered, please choose the phrase, word, action and so on with which you identify most. Give that preference 4 marks. In each category, there are four choices, so you need to allocate 3 marks to your next choice, then 2, and finally 1 mark for the item with which you identify least.

Let us take the first example, where you imagine that you have total freedom to choose between four different jobs, as set out below. In this case, I have chosen social worker (4 marks), followed by researcher (3 marks) followed by writer (2 marks), with administrator bringing up the rear with the final single point.

1. Jobs (examples)

Marks

Researcher	A	3
Administrator	B	1
Writer	C	2
Social worker	D	4

Please complete the form in this way, then fill out the scoring sheet on page 110. To do this, transfer each mark for each set of choices to one of the four categories LD, CC, PF, PC. For example, with the choices made in the example above, the A mark of 3 goes in the LD column, the B mark of 1 goes in the CC column, the C mark of 2 in the PC column and the D mark of 4 in the PF column. Thus, when scoring, find the letter and put the mark corresponding to the letter in the space next to it.

Then, add up the figures in each column, entering the totals at the foot in the spaces provided. Your totals should add up to 120. Finally, draw a line for each total in its respective column in the profile chart on page 111, following the example.

1. Jobs

Marks

Researcher	A	
Administrator	B	
Writer	C	
Social worker	D	

2. Words

Marks

Harmony	A	
Beauty	B	
Intellect	C	
Efficiency	D	

3. Words

Keep
Evaluate
Share
Change

Marks	
A	
B	
C	
D	

4. Words

Idea
Feeling
Organization
Fact

Marks	
A	
B	
C	
D	

5. Phrases

The right answer ⌐D
Safety first Cc
Go for it Pc
Sixth sense PF

Marks	
A	
B	
C	
D	

6. Sayings

Smile and the whole world smiles
Nothing ventured, nothing gained
The facts speak for themselves
Look before you leap

Marks	
A	
B	
C	
D	

7. How someone who does not like you might describe you

Being stuck in the mud
Being as dry as dust
Wearing your heart on your sleeve
Having your head in the clouds

Marks	
A	
B	
C	
D	

8. Attitude to risk

Do you prefer to:

	Marks
A	
B	
C	
D	

take risks — A
share risks — B
avoid risks — C
analyse risks — D

9. Attitude to change

Do you prefer to:

	Marks
A	
B	
C	
D	

analyse and evaluate ideas — A
implement ideas that are practical — B
generate ideas — C
look to see how ideas will affect others — D

10. Actions you take

Do you prefer to:

	Marks
A	
B	
C	
D	

make a new friend — A
change your approach — B
have a debate — C
control a situation — D

11. How you would describe yourself?

	Marks
A	
B	
C	
D	

Practical — A
Rational — B
Friendly — C
Imaginative — D

12. How someone who does not like you might describe you

	Marks
A	
B	
C	
D	

Rebellious — A
Weak — B
Overly cautious — C
Cold — D

Scoring sheet for your questionnaire

Question number	Your Profile			
	LD	CC	PF	PC
1.	A	B	D	C
2.	C	D	A	B
3.	B	A	C	D
4.	D	C	B	A
5.	A	B	D	C
6.	C	D	A	B
7.	B	A	C	D
8.	D	C	B	A
9.	A	B	D	C
10.	C	D	A	B
11.	B	A	C	D
12.	D	C	B	A

Totals —— + —— + —— + —— = 120

UNDERSTANDING CHANGE PREFERENCES

Figure 11.1 sets out the four change preferences and Figure 11.2 explains the model, based on Ned Herrmann's divisions of the brain, and shows what the initials you saw on the scoring sheet stand for.

The first point to make is that, apart from one or two exceptional people, we operate in different modes at different times when experiencing change. However, we may have a strong preference

Your change preference profile

Example

Preference	LD	CC	PF	PC
High 48 42 36				
Moderate 30 24				
Low 18 12				
Score				

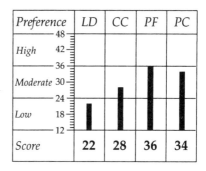

Preference	LD	CC	PF	PC
High 48 42 36				
Moderate 30 24				
Low 18 12				
Score	22	28	36	34

Analyse and evaluate	Explore and discover
Resist and stay in control	Accept and help others

Figure 11.1 *The four change preferences*

for a particular mode, in which case we are likely to rely on that approach most of the time.

Before interpreting the profile as a whole, let us first look at each mode as if we were operating in that mode, and consider what that means in terms of approach.

Let us take an example. We shall use the same example for each mode so that the differences between them can be highlighted. Let us assume that we have been told by the personnel depart-

Internal focus	External focus
LD Logical detached	PC Positive creative
Cautious control CC	People-focused PF
Left brain	Right brain

Intellectual

Emotional

Figure 11.2 *Ned Herrmann's divisions of the brain*

ment that there may be a promotion for us from, say, assistant manager in our section to manager.

Logical detached (LD)

In this mode, we are unemotional and have a rational perspective (see Figure 11.3). We will be interested in the facts of the matter, and the implications, trying to make sense of things. We won't be challenging the nature and dimensions of the change, nor considering the emotional impact on ourselves or others, but, rather, focusing on an analysis of the event and what it means.

As a logical detached person, the promotion makes obvious sense in career progression terms. You would want to find out such things as when the promotion was to occur, why you had been selected, what it meant in terms of extra pay and non-financial benefits; you would want to check that your understanding of the role and responsibilities was clear, whether or not there were any rivals for the job, what the selection process and timing would be, what the probability of getting the job

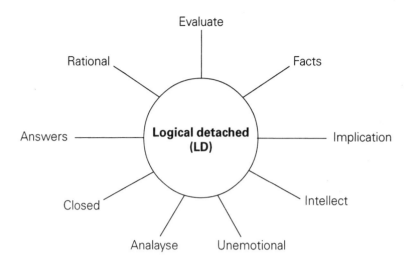

Figure 11.3 *The logical detached approach to change*

would be and so on – all the logical questions. If the answers made sense, you would be happy.

The LD approach is closed in the sense that we accept the change for what it is, then ask the questions that resolve the issues arising from the change.

In real life, we would not stay in this mode throughout, particularly when we first learn about a change. If you have a very high LD score, and there is a big gap between that and the next score, the chances are that you are a very logical, emotionally controlled person, and would react in the way suggested.

Cautious control (CC)

In this mode our reaction is fundamentally emotional, negative and self-centred (see Figure 11.4). We instinctively resist the change because it necessarily disrupts the status quo, with which we are happy. Depending on the nature of the change, we may deny its existence, as can happen with sudden and traumatic changes.

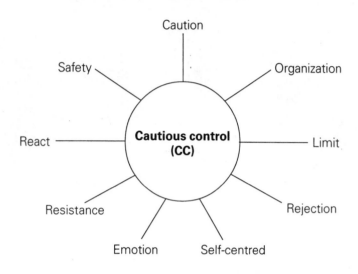

Figure 11.4 *The cautious control approach to change*

We are in a fight to control our environment, under threat from the change. We automatically tend to accentuate the negative, expressing our views logically and, if necessary, illogically. If we fight in vain, and the change is forced upon us, then we try to minimize the damage and maximize the connection to the present and past.

So, if you were a cautious control person and heard about the possible promotion, your instant internal reaction would be 'No thanks!' Politically, that might not be possible to state baldly, and so you might demur, mentioning how happy you are in your current role, and how good you are at that job, or you might try to postpone, suggesting the timing is not quite right – a year or so later, you would absolutely love promotion, or you might go with the 'I don't feel I am quite ready for it, haven't developed the right skills yet' supplementary approach.

However, if your fight is in vain, and you are promoted, then you would have a pragmatic and organized approach so that the new environment would become comfortable as soon as possible.

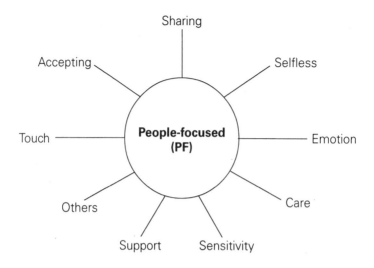

Figure 11.5 *The people-focused approach to change*

People-focused (PF)

In this mode, we tend to accept the change, rather than challenge, explore or resist the experience; we react emotionally rather than intellectually, and our primary focus is not ourselves but others who are affected by the change (see Figure 11.5).

Our emotional needs are likely to be satisfied by sharing the experience as far as possible, thereby gaining support and providing support to those also affected.

Taking the example of the possible promotion, in PF mode, you would be likely to be pleased and want to share the good news with colleagues, friends and relatives. You would be concerned about the impact it would have on all the staff in the section, how they would react to your more senior status in the same department, particularly former peers, who would be put in a subordinate role to you.

Positive creative (PC)

In this mode, we enjoy change, like taking risks and want to be part of the future that change is creating (see Figure 11.6). We tend not to be emotionally involved with the consequences of change on ourselves and others, but are wrapped up in the dynamics of change – full of questions and ideas as we explore the possibilities change brings in its wake.

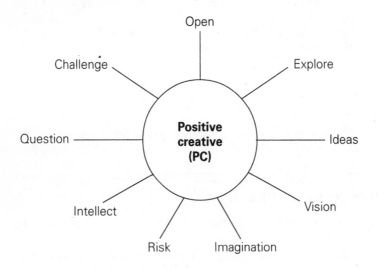

Figure 11.6 *The positive creative approach to change*

Considering the possible promotion, as a PC person, you would be interested in making sure you knew what the job entailed, you would be enthusiastic, you would explore the boundaries and constraints, challenge them, consider new approaches (as, in this instance, you would have a good idea of the current job, as it is held by your boss), new ways of meeting the objectives and new objectives to meet.

In real life, people who only use this mode would probably not get the job! The likely reaction of a boss (to whom, inevitably, a PC person would be talking at some stage) would be negative as such a subordinate seems to question and challenge that boss' approach (this is likely to be the perception of the boss, though not the intention of the subordinate with their PC hat on).

Now that we have looked at each mode, we next consider your own profile and the messages it brings for how you manage change.

UNDERSTANDING YOUR PROFILE

The questionnaire forced you to choose, and so the profile indicates which mode or modes you prefer. The stronger the preference, in relative terms, the more likely you are to adopt the particular preferred mode or modes when experiencing change.

Additionally, *the profile indicates the extent to which you are likely to initiate change.* For instance, if you have a score of, say, 36 or more in PC (positive creative) and 24 or under in CC (cautious control), showing that PC is a strong mode and CC is a weak mode, then you will often be an initiator of change. With the reverse scoring, however, you would maintain the status quo.

We now consider five profiles and highlight the key implications of them. This will help your understanding of the implications of your own profile. The conclusions indicated by the profile were confirmed in one-to-one conversations with the people who produced them (all names have been changed).

Hazel

LD	CC	PF	PC
22	30	**38**	30

I have emboldened the strongest preference and italicized the weakest, which will be a consistent approach throughout these examples.

Hazel's preferred mode is people-focused (PF), with positive creative (PC) and cautious control (CC) in support or secondary. The gap of 8 between PF and PC/CC is significant. The logical detached (LD) approach is only occasionally used.

Hazel appears to fundamentally care for others and be concerned about how others will be affected by change – that is, she is emotionally involved rather than intellectually involved. The total of the 'emotional' scores (CC + PF; 30 + 38 = 68) is significantly higher than the total intellectual scores (LD + PC; 22 + 30 = 52).

Within the emotional side, the desire to be in control and safe is quite strong. This could lead to tension when Hazel's feelings for others and her exciting creative side conflict with the need to stay in control, keep both feet on the ground and connect back to the present and the past.

Within the intellectual side, there is a preference for the possibilities of change and excitement with change itself rather than a detached analysis of the consequences of change.

For Hazel, the kind of change that would be most acceptable to her would need to:

❑ be exciting;
❑ be connected to the past;
❑ ensure that she stays in control;
❑ occur with another person.

Hazel would find it tough to change circumstances without support. The high PF score does indicate that Hazel could be bullied into change by a strong personality with whom she is emotionally involved.

As regards initiating change, the difference between her PC and CC scores is exactly 0, and, in the absence of the involvement of another person (a shared venture), she is unlikely to be very proactive.

Rodney

LD	CC	PF	PC
30	15	**37**	**38**

A difference of one or two points between scores is not significant. We see that Rodney has two preferred modes – people-focused and positive creative, with logical detached in support. There is a very low cautious control score (the minimum possible is 12).

Rodney is an individual who likes change and will often initiate it (the difference between the PC and CC scores is a very large 24). He is happy to involve others or at least one other (high PF). There is a strong intellectual bias (68 – 52 = 16) combining both the creative and evaluative aspects (LD = 30).

With the very low CC score, he would be able to react well to traumatic events by giving and receiving emotional support, using rationalization and the strong PC aspect. He would be able to look beyond and around the event and generate options and approaches outside the limitations and perceived realities, which would bind someone with a high CC score.

However, another aspect of the low CC score is that there may well be occasions when Rodney is controlled by, rather than controlling, change. The low perceived preference for control can result in the absence of control.

Mabel

LD	CC	PF	PC
35	**37**	*24*	*24*

Mabel's preferred modes are logical detached and cautious control, with a significant gap between those modes and the less used people-focused and positive creative. Mabel doesn't like change – she resists it and tries to control her environment. She rarely initiates change and is not inclined to be very supportive of others experiencing it.

When change does occur, she will try to rationalize it (LD = 35) rather than challenge or modify it, and focus on producing order from the temporary chaos created. There is a certain brittleness in this profile, with the emphasis on the self, the past and detached logical thought.

The kind of change that would be most acceptable to Mabel would be gradual, strongly connected to the present and the past and where she felt in control throughout and could understand and accept the logic of it all.

Unlike Rodney, Mabel would find traumatic change particularly difficult to handle. This is, in fact, because she suffered traumatic change in the past, which has had a significant and, to date, permanent impact on her approach to change.

Joanne

LD	CC	PF	PC
19	*31*	**36**	**34**

Joanne has people-focused and positive creative as preferred modes, with cautious control in strong support, and very little preference for logical detached.

All the scores, apart from LD, are in the moderate range, though at the top end. There is an emotional bias (67 compared with 53) and a preference for exploring rather than evaluating change. The moderate CC score – only 5 less than PF – implies that she would tend to initiate change that was not too radical; evolutionary rather than revolutionary.

The low LD score suggests that she does not think through the impact and implications of change and could be caught out by unanticipated consequences. The PF score indicates support for others also involved in change, and that she has a desire to share the experience.

Reaction to traumatic change would be quite testing (CC = 31), but would be helped by the PF and PC strengths.

Karl

LD	CC	PF	PC
32	*26*	30	**32**

All Karl's scores are in the moderate range, and the gap between the highest and lowest is only 6.

There is a slight intellectual bias (64 compared to 56) and a moderate difference between PC and CC of 6. Karl, like Joanne, will tend to initiate change of an evolutionary nature rather than the risky or revolutionary sort. Unlike Joanne, when experiencing the change, he is likely to evaluate the impact and implications, as well as explore the possibilities and challenge the boundaries.

However, as implied by the scores, Karl is unlikely to push or challenge too far or need a lot of control, and will only provide moderate support to others involved.

Before looking at the team dimension, it is worth considering if there is any gender difference in our change preferences.

COMPARING MEN AND WOMEN

While it is helpful to look at the absolute scores and the implications of differences and which modes we prefer, additional value can be gained by comparing our profiles with the norms, combining and averaging the scores of all those who have filled in the assessment.

There are two such profiles as men and women are not identical, on average, for this particular assessment. Before looking at these, I would enter a caveat about preferences. We do not always do what we would like to do. There are many factors that can create a gap between our desired and actual approaches to change. Four key factors are:

❑   the nature of a given task or project;
❑   the level of stress;
❑   the individual relationship and the level, such as 'boss' or 'subordinate';
❑   aspiration without actuality.

A preference does not indicate competence or skill. In some situations, we may intend to behave in a certain way, but the behaviour we manifest may not match that intention exactly. Equally, the impact on someone else may be different from what we intended.

The female profile

LD	CC	PF	PC
27	28	**35**	30

We see here LD and CC scores that are nearly balanced, a preference for PF and a moderate PC score. There is a preference for emotional (PF + CC = 63) rather than intellectual responses (LD + PC = 57), a difference of 6. The small difference between CC and PC suggests that, on average, changes initiated will be small and connected rather than discontinuous, with a preference for a partner (high PF).

The male profile

LD	CC	PF	PC	
31	26	30	33	Male profile
27	28	35	30	Female profile
4	(2)	(5)	3	Difference

There is a greater preference for a logically detached approach to change, slightly less resistance to it, less concern with the impact on others and greater desire for positive exploration in the male profile than is the case in the female profile.

There is a reversal of the females' intellectual/emotional balance, with LD + PC = 64 and PF + CC = 56, a difference of 8 for the males.

The gap of 7 between PC and CC in the male profile suggests that men are more the initiators of change than women.

Note that this is, of course, on average. There will be many profiles of individuals where there is no 'gender' bias.

THE IMPACT ON RELATIONSHIPS

Differences in profiles are not initially perceived as a positive by most people. How do you think someone high in CC sees someone high in PC, and vice versa? How do you think someone high in LD sees someone high in PF, and vice versa?

You can either guess the profile of key players in your working environment (not too difficult) or get them to fill in the questionnaire. You will then see why you get on well with some people (those with a similar profile) and not with others (those with different profiles).

Where there is difference, the results can be used as a basis for improving the relationship and trying to harness the difference to add value, which is always potentially there.

PLAYING TO STRENGTHS

There is always a danger that we start feeling dissatisfied with ourselves when we start 'objectively' considering how we approach change or the conclusions of any assessment or questionnaire. This is assuming that we don't react to any feeling of emerging conscious incompetence with the CC response: 'What a load of rubbish. I reject all this nonsense.'

In fact, the higher your CC score, the more likely it is that you have, or are moving into, a rejection mode. If you have a high LD score, you may well be finding flaws in the instrument, where you perceive a logical inconsistency, and starting the rejection process – that is, there may be rejection on both logical and emotional grounds.

In fact, those who have a high LD/CC combination may well not be reading this section at all! This is a pity, because there is neither a right nor wrong answer, nor a right nor wrong change preference mode.

A key to creating growth from change is to develop an integrated approach using all the responses, as each is needed at different times and phases. This is particularly difficult when we are reacting to change and is much easier when we initiate change. I thus conclude this section by highlighting the strengths of each approach.

Logical detached (LD)

The ability to stand back, be objective and analyse and evaluate the implications of change is essential to achieving growth. Imposing the necessary discipline of facts and information, and curbing the excess of the improbable, are vital components in this process.

Cautious control (CC)

There are considerable strengths in this preference. Change is more acceptable, generally, if it is delivered in stages and is strongly connected to the past. In fact, the Japanese, who are very conservative as a nation, have used this preference very well in developing continuous improvement cultures.

Paradoxically, we could argue that the CC preference is too low in many organizations in the West, and needs to be developed to obtain continuous improvement cultures.

Provided the strong CC individual recognizes the need for improvement rather than radical change, he or she will be very useful in both making and selling the connections to the status quo.

People-focused (PF)

Change almost invariably involves others as well as ourselves. The ability to recognize how others are affected, listen to and understand their concerns and support them through change smoothes the path for all of us.

Positive creative (PC)

Change is never set in concrete. A creative, exploring and challenging approach to change can significantly improve both its nature and the outcomes for the better.

DEVELOPING COMPENSATION STRATEGIES

In the absence of effective teamworking, it is worth thinking what strategies you can put in place to reduce or compensate for weaknesses.

For instance, my own profile is high PC, quite strong PF, moderate LD and very low CC. I like my profile, but I recognize that I make too many changes too quickly. Whenever possible, I pair up with someone who has the strengths I lack. Failing that, I force myself to pause – to deliberately seek out the CC, and never make any significant change until I have slept on it.

UNDERSTANDING THE TEAM DIMENSION

If you are a team leader or, for that matter, a team member, and can persuade your colleagues to complete the change preference questionnaire, you can obtain some useful insights into the overall orientation towards change management as well as explanations for any subgroupings or alienation of individuals that might exist. The focus of any group exercise should be on how to work together to be more effective and what strategies to put in place to remove any individual alienation or subgrouping so that the team performs more effectively and relationships in the team are more supportive in the light of recognition and understanding of differences that always have the potential to add value.

We shall work through an example taken from real life, as well as leaving a blank field diagram for you to fill in for your team.

For simplicity, I have allocated the letters A to F for the six team members. Figure 11.7 sets out their scores for the change preference questionnaire and carries out the mathematics.

By subtracting the CC score from the PC score, we get the net score indicating the degree of proactivity towards change management.

By subtracting the LD score from the PF score, we get the net score indicating the degree of people focus/positive emotional as compared to the logical approach to change.

The two net scores (for example, for A these are 16 and 12) can be plotted on the field diagram for the team, with each individual having a unique position on that diagram (see Figure 11.8). Each quadrant indicates an overall approach, as follows.

	CC	PC	PC-CC	LD	PF	PF-LD
A	20	36	+16	26	38	+12
B	23	24	+1	33	40	+7
C	19	42	+23	33	26	-7
D	39	19	-20	41	21	-20
E	41	31	-10	34	14	-20
F	26	32	+6	24	38	+16

Figure 11.7 *The team dimension to change preferences*

Emotional

The net of CC and PF. Those in this quadrant have an instinctive emotional response combining an emotionally cautious approach in terms of personal reaction with a desire to help others. Such an individual would need a lot of emotional support and to be sold benefits from a personal perspective.

Right-brained

The net of PC and PF. This quadrant is home to those who are proactive, positive and challenging as well as supportive of others. These are useful people to have in the team, but may lack sufficient caution and not think through the logical implications and consequences. They are good team motivators, but, without balancing forces, could lead everyone over the cliff edge.

Intellectual

The net of PC and LD. People in this quadrant are great at working out what changes to make and how to implement them – excellent strategists – but can fail to convince or motivate others and create unanticipated resistance among the troops.

Left-brained

The net of CC and LD. Those inhabiting this quadrant can point out all the problems and flaws – a necessary talent for effective change management – but will tend to be too analytical and conservative so that too little tends to be done too late. They are unlikely to grasp the big picture easily.

FILLING IN A FIELD DIAGRAM

We have put the six team members shown in Figure 11.7 on the field diagram shown in Figure 11.8, and the results mirrored real life.

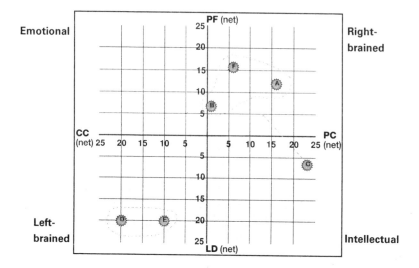

Figure 11.8 *Field diagram for a team*

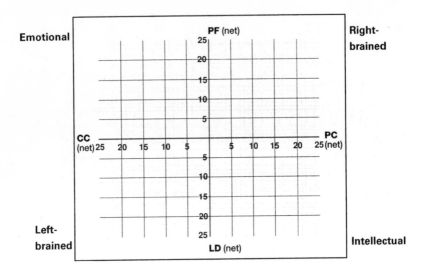

Figure 11.9 *Field diagram for your team*

❑ C was the rebel, in danger of losing his job as he was isolated, though trying to gravitate towards the subgroup B, F and A.

❑ B, F and A formed a natural alliance and were the pressure to drive through necessary change, but were thwarted by the combination of D and E.

❑ D and E also formed a natural alliance, with E being the group leader with higher status. He was a senior manager in a very conservative insurance company, struggling with the need to change. He held endless meetings, which he dominated with D's support, that went on for ages and led to a number of action plans that were never implemented as no one was motivated to do so.

What change took place was completely outside the main team meetings and executed by the B, F and A group.

In terms of improvement, B, who was closest to the rest of the team, needed to have a coordinator role, with a tightly controlled process to manage change effectively.

Use the blank field diagram shown in Figure 11.9 to plot the members of your own team.

12

REVIEWING AND PLANNING

In this chapter, we provide a summary of the key points of each chapter, and conclude with a set of questions that, in answering them, will help you plan to be a more effective leader.

SUMMARIZING THE KEY POINTS

In this section, we summarize the key points of all 11 chapters.

Understanding effective leadership

❑ Leadership is one of four work roles: leadership, followership, technical and administration.

❑ As we spend a significant amount of time in the leadership role, it is worth planning how to be effective in it.

❑ Effective leadership and ineffective leadership are determined by behaviours and actions that anyone is capable of.

❑ Effective leaders focus on their followers – putting the followers' work into context, developing them, leading by example and providing support.

Maximizing flexibility and choice

❑ We need to develop the right attitude – believing in the vital importance of our leadership role, recognizing that we should not follow the traditional model of making all the decisions and being in charge, believe in our own capability to be effective and develop a positive attitude to those we lead.

❏ By means of a questionnaire, you can discover the extent to which you see yourself as supporting, controlling or team-oriented. By getting a colleague to complete the identical questionnaire on yourself, you can determine the extent and direction of any gaps in perception.

❏ You can determine your leadership style and your colleagues' perception of your style. The four styles are S1 = tell, S2 = coach, S3 = support, S4 = delegate.

❏ Leadership should vary according to the situation and competence/confidence of the follower.

❏ Effective development of a follower can be seen as a progression through the four styles of leadership.

Eliminating perception gaps

❏ There are two gaps in perception: the manifestation of our behaviour can be different to what we consciously intended (gap 1) and, even if it is how we intended it to be, the impact on the follower can be different from the manifestation (gap 2).

❏ The causes of gap 1 are reacting to stress, a subconscious desire to criticize or poor communication. Specific solutions are to avoid hasty interventions, use the assertive pause to deliberately examine our subconscious motivations, avoid jargon, and ensure that the follower has understood what we are communicating.

❏ The causes of gap 2 are entering the wrong environment, poor listening skills of the follower, and the follower having developed a fixed mind-set towards us. Solutions are, again, to avoid hasty interventions and to ask the follower to recap so that they are made to understand. For the fixed mind-set, adopt the generic solution.

❏ The generic solution is to create the right environment with planned meetings and regular reviews. This is especially necessary to avoid the cumulator, which is when there is a combination of a cause or causes on both gaps, leading to a shouting match or dismissal of the follower.

Motivating staff

- ❑ Our motivation will depend on how high our self-esteem is.
- ❑ Those factors that meet our physiological and safety needs dissatisfy if there are absent, but do not motivate if they are present.
- ❑ Motivators are not derived from the context of the job, but the content. Motivational factors come from the degree of responsibility, achievement and autonomy we can develop, how participative and friendly the environment is, the extent to which we receive recognition and praise, and how much we can learn and develop.
- ❑ As leaders, there is a priority of strategies we can use to motivate our followers. Specifically, these are to promote effective feedback, show flexibility in our leadership style and be more supportive, delegate effectively, allow risk-taking, train and develop, generate high expectations, provide goals and acknowledge achievement.

Questioning effectively

- ❑ The key to establishing good relationships with followers and developing them effectively is to ask open questions – 'What?', 'Why?' and 'How?' – and avoid closed questions, which only lead to 'Yes' or 'No' answers.
- ❑ We tend to avoid open questions because of our education, our psychology and sheer ignorance.
- ❑ The key strategies to ensure that we have effective conversations with our followers (or, for that matter, partner or customers) are to think first, think open question, avoid leading or loaded questions, avoid 'logical', closed alternatives, use perceptive, probing questions, use the right wording, keep questions simple, keep questions single, provide answers when asked, and put in lots of practice.

Listening actively

❏ Like effective questioning, effective or active listening can be difficult because talkers are rewarded. We can think we are more important or more knowledgeable than the follower, we can think faster than the follower speaks and so distract ourselves, we can have a negative mind-set regarding the follower, and the follower can be a poor speaker.

❏ We can identify poor listening by observing body language. There are six categories: aggressive listening, which can be deliberate or accidental, passive listening, listening interruptus, logical listening, arrogant listening and nervous listening.

❏ To become better listeners, we need to be committed to the act of listening, objective, suspend judgement, check for understanding, use positive body language with the appropriate facial expression, not make gestures and have a good body posture, use words both to reflect back key phrases and murmurs to show interest, and appreciate silence – the power of the pause.

Developing creativity

❏ A very powerful way of increasing individual, and particularly group, creativity is to deploy the group discovery technique (GDT). This requires that we separate out exploration from evaluation, ensuring that there is no criticism of any idea by anyone during exploration, with non-verbal as well as verbal criticism banned. It also helps if each tries to develop and grow the ideas emerging so that there is genuine discovery and group synergy.

❏ There are various powerful question combinations that help develop ideas and solve problems. 'Why not?'/'How?' – as exemplified by the Alaskan Electricity Company example – is a way to reach a specific solution to a given problem. 'Why?'/'Why?' is cause and effect analysis, which can uncover a number of causes and, hence, solution areas. 'How?'/'How?' is the traditional creative thinking approach, leading to different levels of thought and a series of solutions to a given problem. 'What?'/'How?' (force field analysis) is a structured technique to implement any change, and 'What?'/'Why?' is a way of checking for false assumptions before solving the problem.

Improving staff performance

❑ A visual image is used to help us prioritize. An elephant is defined as a core business goal and an ant as an unimportant, trivial work activity.

❑ Focusing on key areas is achieved first of all by 'catching the elephants' – defining the goals, setting SMART objectives and interim milestones, and determining the activities to be carried out.

❑ Prioritizing our elephants and ants, urgent and non-urgent, is a powerful way of focusing work activity.

❑ Ants should be eliminated by such strategies as ignoring them, delegating them or reducing the impact by managing follower expectations, using systems and grouping them.

❑ With a performance measurement in place, which can be reported on a monthly basis, the leader is in a position to monitor the follower's performance on a regular basis, and take appropriate action if performance is below, around or above the agreed standards.

Building a team

❑ An effective team is the most powerful way to develop the individual and maximize business performance.

❑ A picture of what an effective team looks like can easily be created by reversing all the negative factors we have experienced at meetings in the workplace.

❑ The key strategies for building a high-performance team are self-belief, belief in the potential of each team member, using the GDT, identifying and playing to individuals' strengths to help the team develop, meeting regularly, using the power of process, promoting feedback based on the principle of 'promoting discovery', developing a team vision and values, and remembering that the leader's key role is coordinator of process, not controller of people.

Reacting to change

❑ By reflecting on experiences of sudden change, perceived initially negatively, the reaction curve was discovered.

❑ The key phases are shock and denial, resistance and then dawning awareness, anger and blame, acceptance and regret (the low point) followed by strength, recognition, discovery and integration, so that self-esteem, confidence and competence are higher at the end than before the change occurred or was announced.

❑ The first step towards maximizing gain is for the leader to reach the sunny uplands using the assertive pause to control emotions, ensuring full understanding of the thinking behind the change, seeking support from a colleague, partner or friend, trying to envision success after implementation and accentuating all the positive aspects.

❑ The leader is then in a position to help each follower by giving a full explanation, sharing his/her vision, accentuating the positive, providing support, acknowledging emotions, answering all questions, providing time and encouraging involvement in how the change will be implemented.

❑ With a team, a sudden change perceived negatively will threaten a complete breakdown of the team unless the leader, having controlled his/her own emotions, intervenes decisively by calling a meeting, acknowledging the negative emotions and rapidly moving the group towards cause and effect analysis – focusing the group on solving any problems the change has created.

Understanding your change preferences

❑ Four approaches to change are examined by means of a simple self-assessment.

❏ In logical detached (LD) mode, we are emotionally uninvolved, accept the change and analyse and evaluate its implications.

❏ In cautious control (CC) mode, we tend to reject or resist change, control its impact and connect strongly to the past.

❏ In people-focused (PF) mode, we tend to accept the change, be emotionally involved and focus on giving support to others affected.

❏ In positive creative (PC) mode, we are positive towards change and like to explore, challenge and alter the dynamics of change.

❏ The combination of scores provides our change preference profile, showing which approaches we prefer.

❏ The greater the gap between the PC and the CC modes, the more likely we are to be initiators of change. If our CC score is higher than our PC score, we are likely to be maintainers of the status quo.

❏ Men tend to prefer a more logical approach, are less negative, provide less support and are more likely to initiate change than women.

❏ The profiles can be used to see where and why there are 'personality' clashes.

❏ Gaining effective growth from change requires all approaches to be deployed at different times in the cycle.

❏ We should recognize the strengths in each approach and the strengths in each of our profiles.

❏ In the absence of an effective team, it is worth devising and implementing strategies to compensate for weaknesses.

❏ The CC approach may well be undervalued. Provided there is the ability to accept the need for improvement rather than radical change, a CC approach is the key to developing a continuous improvement culture and deriving value from the past, which should be retained in the future.

❏ The field diagram for a team is useful for assessing the overall team approach to change management as well as the positioning and relationships of the individuals in the team.

PLANNING TO BE A MORE EFFECTIVE LEADER

We have a methodology in place for this – a set of questions to guide your thinking. So, I leave you with the key questions and space for your own answers.

1. What is your goal(s)?

2. What is your SMART objective(s)?

3. What is your interim milestone(s)?

4. What actions do you need to take, in what order, to reach the first milestone(s)?

Good luck.

Rupert Eales-White

BIBLIOGRAPHY AND RECOMMENDED READING

Adair, J (1988) *Effective Leadership*, Pan, London.

Belbin, Meredith R (1981) *Management Teams: Why They Succeed or Fail*, Butterworth-Heinemann, Oxford.

Bennis, W (1989) *On Becoming a Leader*, Addison-Wesley Publishing Company, USA.

Blanchard, K and Johnson, S (1983) *The One Minute Manager*, Fontana, London.

Drucker, P F (1967) *The Effective Executive*, Heinemann Professional Publishing, London.

Eales-White, R (1992) *The Power of Persuasion: Improving Your Performance and Leadership Skills*, Kogan Page, London.

Eales-White, R (1994) *Creating Growth from Change: How You React, Develop and Grow*, McGraw-Hill, Maidenhead.

Eales-White, R (1996) *How to be a Better Team-builder*, Kogan Page, London.

Eales-White, R (1997) *Ask the Right Question – Tips and Techniques to Transform Your Key Skills and Relationships*, McGraw-Hill, Maidenhead.

Harrison, R (1991) *Humanising Change: a Culture-Based Approach*, Harrison Associates, USA.

Harvey-Jones, J (1988) *Making it Happen: Reflections on Leadership*, Fontana/Collins, London.

Herrmann, N (1988) *The Creative Brain*, Brain Books, North Carolina, USA.

Kelley, R (1988) 'In Praise of Followers', *Harvard Business Review* No. 88606, November–December.

Mackay, I (1984) *A Guide to Listening*, Bacie, London.

Marguerison, C and McCann R (1990), *Team Management: Practical New Approaches*, WH Allen & Co, London.

Montebello, A and Buzzotta, V (1993) 'Work Teams that Work', *Training and Development Journal*, March 1993.

Pease, A (1981) *Body Language: How to Read Others' Thoughts by Their Gestures*, Sheldon Press, London.

Peters, T (1987), *Thriving on Chaos: Handbook for a Management Revolution*, Knopf, New York.

Van Maurik, J (1994) *Discovering the Leader in You*, McGraw-Hill, Maidenhead.

Van Maurik, J (1996) *The Portable Leader*, McGraw-Hill, Maidenhead.

INDEX

Further How to be a Better... titles

How to Be a Better Interviewer
Margaret Dale

Packed with proven interview tips and mini case studies, this practical guide will show you how to pick the right person for the job every time. Topics include how to:

- choose the right interview techniques
- prepare for interview
- put the interviewee at their ease
- give feedback to unsuccessful candidates.

£8.99 • Paperback • 0 7494 1902 4
128 pages

How to Be a Better Negotiator
John Mattock and Jons Ehrenborg

The authors offer a user-friendly approach to understanding the techniques for effective negotiation in everyday business situations. Topics include how to:

- gain and regain control without being aggressive
- set ambitious goals and reach them through creative bargaining
- grow in confidence as success leads to success.

£8.99 • Paperback • 0 7494 2093 6
128 pages

How to Be Better at Motivating People
John Allan

Packed with examples and checklists, this easy-to-use guide will show you how to motivate all kinds of teams and individuals more effectively. Includes how to:

- motivate all types of people
- motivate both individuals and teams
- motivate your boss.

£8.99 • Paperback • 0 7494 1913 X
128 pages

How to Be a Better Teambuilder
Rupert Eales-White

Improve your team's performances through better motivation, empowerment and control with the practical advice offered in this book. Core topics include:

- developing effective questioning and listening skills in each member
- team motivation
- developing an environment of humour, challenge an support.

£8.99 • Paperback • 0 7494 1912 1
128 pages

KOGAN PAGE

Further | How to be a Better... titles

Further How to be a Better... titles

How to Be Better at Creativity
Geoffrey Petty

By working through the techniques and questionnaires offered here anyone can improve their creative thinking skills with the author's unique six-step model:

Inspiration - spontaneously generating ideas

Claification - focusing on what you are trying to achieve

Distillation - deciding which of your ideas work

Perspiration - pushing your ideas to completion

Incubation - harnessing the power of your unconcious

Evaluation - considering how to improve your work, and learn from it.

£8.99 • Paperback • 0 7494 2167 3
128 pages

How to Be a Better Communicator
Sandy McMillan

A personal, no-nonsense guide to getting your message across clearly and unambiguously every time. This book will teach you how to:

- get your point across clearly and precisely
- understand the importance of listening
- plan, prepare and deliver a talk or report
- deal with face-to-face situations

£8.99 • Paperback • 0 7494 2025 1
128 pages

 KOGAN PAGE

How to Be a Better Time Manager
Jane Smith

Written in an accessible style, this book provides all the practical advice you need to work more effectively, showing you how to:

- plan your time
- prioritise your tasks
- deal effectively with interruptions
- use new technology to your advantage.

£8.99 • Paperback • 0 7494 2375 7
128 pages

How to Be a Better Decision Maker
Alan Barker

This guide shows you how to combine logic and intuition in the quest for more effective decision-making. The book includes:

- improve your decision making
- commit to decisions and gain others' commitment
- avoid being overwhelmed with information
- evaluate the outcomes of your decisions.

£8.99 • Paperback • 0 7494 1950 4
128 pages

How to Be a Better Problem Solver
Michael Stevens

This practical book will help you improve your problem-solving skills and enable you to:

- recognise and define problems
- arrive at practical and effective solutions
- solve problems in a group
- apply problem-solving tools to everyday situations.

£8.99 • Paperback • 0 7494 1901 6
128 pages